STOCK MARKET INVESTING FOR BEGINNERS

STEP-BY-STEP GUIDE TO BUILD WEALTH, AVOID COMMON MISTAKES, AND SECURE YOUR FINANCIAL FUTURE

JORDAN BLAKE

INTRODUCTION

Navigating the stock market can seem like a daunting task for beginners, filled with complex jargon, fluctuating numbers, and a seemingly endless stream of investment strategies. However, the essence of successful investing lies not in mastering every technical detail, but in building a solid foundation of understanding and confidence. This book is crafted with that mission in mind: to transform the overwhelming landscape of stock market investing into a structured, step-by-step journey that anyone can embark on with clarity and purpose.

For many newcomers, the stock market appears as an exclusive club, accessible only to finance experts or those with significant capital. The reality, however, is that investing is a skill that can be learned and refined over time, regardless of one's starting point. This guide is designed to demystify the process, breaking down the barriers of entry and equipping you with the tools and knowledge necessary to make informed decisions. Focusing on practical steps and real-world applications aims to empower you to take control of your financial future.

Throughout the pages, you will find clear explanations of key concepts, from understanding the basic types of investments such as stocks, ETFs, and mutual funds, to more advanced topics like portfolio diversification and risk management. We will also address common pitfalls that beginners face, such as the myths surrounding investing and the emotional traps that can lead to poor decision-making. By debunking these misconceptions, the book provides a realistic view of what it takes to succeed in the stock market.

Moreover, this guide emphasizes the importance of setting personalized financial goals and developing an investment strategy that aligns with your unique circumstances and aspirations. Whether you aim to save for retirement, build a college fund, or grow your wealth over time, the strategies outlined here are adaptable to your needs.

In addition to foundational knowledge, practical tools are provided to assist you in your investing journey. From creating a watchlist and evaluating stocks to setting up automated investments, these resources are designed to simplify the process and help you build a routine that fits seamlessly into your life. The goal is not just to teach you how to invest, but to nurture a mindset of continuous learning and growth.

Join a community of like-minded individuals who are also learning to navigate the stock market, sharing experiences, and supporting each other in the pursuit of financial independence. With the right mindset and tools at your disposal, you can confidently step into the world of investing and secure your financial future.

Table of Contents

Chapter 1: Understanding the Basics of Investing

Defining Stocks and Bonds

The backbone of the financial markets is stocks and bonds, each with a different purpose and reaching out to different customers. One should learn about these tools as any newcomer to the world of investments, since these are the basic building blocks in a diversified investment portfolio.

Stocks, also known as equities, represent ownership of a company. As you buy a stock, you are actually buying a part of that business, and that makes you entitled to the profits and assets of that business. Stocks are exchanged, and stock prices vary depending on the performance of the company, the moods of investors, and the general economy. The main charm of cards is that they have a growth likelihood. In the past, equities have shown a greater rate of returns than the other asset classes at the expense of being more volatile and risky. Stock investors are usually investing to get capital gains, dividends, or both. Such types of stocks of stable companies as Apple or Coca-Cola are called blue-chip stocks, and their main advantages are their stability and constant dividend, which makes them attractive to risk-averse investors. In contrast, growth stocks, such as Tesla, appeal to people who prefer to take a risk in exchange for better earnings.

Bonds, on the other hand, are debt instruments. By buying a bond, you will, in effect, lend money to the issuer of the bond, which may be a corporation, municipality, or government. The issuer, in exchange, guarantees to pay you at regular intervals interest and to repay the principal amount at the time of its maturity. Bonds have been regarded as less risky compared to stocks since they pay income steadily and are supported by the creditworthiness of the issuer in most instances. The safest are the government bonds, e.g., the U.S. Treasuries, since the state can always back them with taxes on the population. Corporate bonds are relatively riskier securities than government bonds, but have higher yields to hedge the risk of default.

Bonds and stocks differ in risk and return profiles in many ways. Stocks are easily affected by market changes, and their prices usually vary significantly, depending on such drivers as earnings updates, sector trends, and economic indicators. It is this volatility that can open up to both the possibility of huge profits as well as huge losses. Bonds are, however, more stable and offer predictable cash flow. They especially become appealing in times of economic duress and have greater security than equities, as they do not respond to economic fluctuations.

The investors can use a combination of bonds and stocks to diversify their portfolios and therefore obtain a premium relationship between risk and reward. The equity-to-bond ratio in the portfolio usually depends on the risk that an investor is able to take, the objectives of the investor, and the period as well. The younger investors may focus more on stocks, as those are likely to grow over the years, and they have more years to hold them through volatile periods. On the other hand, investors who are close to retirement may seek stability and income from bonds, as the capital is maintained and the investor earns regular returns.

Conclusively, stocks and bonds are a part and parcel of the financial markets, with each having a specific mission in the investment strategy. Bonds help to earn a stable income through interest, whereas stocks give one the chance of owning into a growing company with prospects of a dividend payout. Both types of assets are often contained in a well-diversified portfolio, depending on the needs of the individual and his or her tolerance of risk.

The Role of the Stock Market

The stock market is an ever-changing place in the complex world of finance, and all the factors are united to form a broad network of economic activity. The stock market is basically a market whereby investors purchase and sell stocks in publicly listed companies, which helps in the flow of money that helps in the growth of businesses and the economy.

The stock market is an important element of the economy as it gives companies an avenue to raise funds in exchange for granting ownership to the investors. It is this capital that is required so that the companies are able to grow their operations, invest in newer projects, and eventually have some benefits in terms of growth in the economy. Instead, the stock market appeals to investors since they have the potential to receive returns on their investments in terms of dividends and gains of the stock market.

Furthermore, the stock market acts as a barometer of the whole state of the economy. It exhibits the perception of the economic conditions, performance of the companies, and future economic outlook by the investors. Increasing stock prices are a sign of confidence and optimism with respect to the effects on the economy by investors. On the flip side, when the stock market goes down, it creates macroeconomic uncertainty, and it also indicates a reduction in corporate profits.

The other important aspect is liquidity, which is offered through the stock market. It enables investors to buy or sell shares easily, and therefore enables investors to sell their investments easily in the form of cash. Such liquidity is critical for the smooth running of the financial system and for the confidence of the investors.

Also, the stock market enhances transparency and accountability. The financial information of any publicly traded company has to be disclosed frequently, and analysts, investors, and regulators study such disclosure. This openness assists in ensuring that there is a fair and efficient market, with prices being subject to all forms of information on the market, thereby minimizing chances of fraud and market manipulation.

The stock market is also educational in the sense that it enables people to learn the concepts of investment and the need to plan for finance. Through the market, investors will get to understand matters such as risk management, diversification, and how occurrences in the economy will affect their portfolio. This kind of knowledge helps them in decision-making regarding their future finances.

Moreover, the stock market can be innovative as it offers ground to new and emergent corporations where they raise their capital. This financing source is vital, especially to startups or small firms that are unable to raise other conventional funds. The stock market helps advance technology and diversify the economy by helping these companies grow and develop.

In a nutshell, the stock market is the backbone of the financial system, which has a complex role in the economy. It gives a facility through which companies are able to raise capital, it gives the individual an avenue to invest, it portrays economic status, and it gives transparency and accountability. It is an important part of the global financial system that ensures economic growth and new developments because the stock market contributes to the effective distribution of resources.

Key Terms and Concepts

To understand the stock market, the first step would be to master its terminology and concepts. These cornerstones equip one with the instruments to traverse and understand the multi-faceted financial world. In the center of stock market investments are different varieties of securities, which are representations of assets or debt ownership. The ownership in a company is represented by stocks or equities, which entitle shareholders to their share of assets and income of a corporation. Bonds are, however, just debt instruments issued by corporations or governments to repay the amount of money plus interest later in the future.

One more important notion is the stock market, which is the place where the selling and purchasing of securities is made possible. These transactions are done through exchanges such as the New York Stock Exchange (NYSE) and NASDAQ, where there is always transparency and liquidity of the market. Every security system has a ticker symbol, which is actually a series of letters that denote the company in the exchange.

Knowledge of the kind of stock orders is imperative to an investor. A market order refers to a request to purchase or sell a stock at its current rate, which is offered instantaneously. On the other hand, a limit order establishes the highest or the lowest price you are prepared to purchase or sell. Stop-loss orders are applied to ensure against great losses by selling a particular stock when it hits a defined price.

The notions of bull and bear markets characterize the overall direction of the stock prices. A bull market is one in which prices are rising and investors are optimistic, and a bear market is one in which prices are declining and there is usually a lot of pessimism. These trends are important to the investor as they enable one to invest in the right direction and utilize their portfolio.

A risk management strategy that entails combining a broad range of investments in a portfolio is known as diversification. The reason is that a diversified portfolio will have more returns compared to individual investments present in the portfolio and will be at a lower risk. This concept can be summarized as well by the saying, one should not put all the eggs in the same basket.

Investors should also know about dividends, which are payments given by a corporation to the shareholders, and in most cases, they are distributed as a profit of the company. Dividends allow a consistent flow of income, and they are also an indicator of a company's solvency.

Examples of valuation ratios, such as price to earnings (P/E), are critical indicators when determining the worth of a stock. P/E ratio is a ratio of a company's share price to earnings per share, which provides an idea of whether the share is overpriced or underpriced.

Also, it is essential to realize the gains and the risks involved in investment. Risk is defined as the possibility of losing part or the entire original investment, and reward is defined as the profit of the investment. It is in the process of balancing these aspects that informed decisions are taken concerning the allocation of assets and the strategy to adopt regarding investments.

Lastly, investing and investing technologies have allowed people to direct their investment portfolios easily. Robo-advisors are automated investing services that offer algorithmically-based financial planning (typically with little or no human oversight), offering efficient portfolio management.

With the understanding of these main terms and notions, a newcomer is able to create a clear background to proceed with further training and effective investment in the stock market. Such information gives people the capacity to make informed choices, match their investments to their financial aim, and make informed choices on the complicated world of the market with confidence.

The Importance of Investing Early

The concept of early investing has deeper meanings to every person who seeks to ensure his or her financial stability in the future. The sooner one begins to invest, the longer he or she is able to access the force of compounding, which can really multiply the value of their investments in the long run.

Compounding refers to the practice in which the returns on an investment (gains made on the amounts of investment plus the interests gained on the same) gain interest as well. The potential to create a large amount of wealth can be realized through this exponential growth.

The earlier you begin to invest, the more time your investments have to multiply. This long time will allow your money more chances to work and earn more chances to exceed returns. In other words, when you invest in your 20s, you still have many decades ahead of you to let the short-term ups and downs of the market pass, and at the same time, enjoy the historical upswing of stocks in the long term. Such forbearance and time benefit can counter the effects of the immediate market fluctuations.

Besides, starting to invest at a young age can stimulate the acquisition of self-disciplined financial behaviors. With a habit of saving and investing through an occasional contribution of income to investments, one may develop a habit of doing it, which may affect financial success during the rest of one's life. The habit not only assists in the act of accumulating wealth but also in developing a feeling of financial security and independence.

The earlier the investment, the more flexibility there is to invest in something more risky, which may be advantageous to growth. The youths tend to have a wide time frame and can thus salvage losses that may be incurred due to a market crash.

This implies that they can invest in more risky and higher-rewarding assets, which have the potential to fetch a higher reward in the long term. As they near retirement age, the investment portfolio may then be changed to use more conservative investments so that the wealth gained may be intact.

In addition, early preparation means more financial planning. The long-term investors also have the advantage of planning long term and steadily working to realize their projections, whether saving to purchase a house, a child's education, or retirement. This prudence and precaution may cause wiser and less worrying financial actions.

The other opportunity for early investing, where a person learns and improves, is another crucial point to be considered. Early investors can learn more and take their time on how to respond to situations, even change their tactics, and even gain more financial knowledge. This learning curve might be vital in the stock market and decision-making based on the trade.

Also, one may enjoy an inflation cushion by investing early. With time, inflation destroys the purchasing power of money. Through investing in an asset that tends to be affected by inflation in a situation where it will be able to overcome inflation, that is, stocks, you will be able to safeguard your wealth as well as your standard of living in the future.

The significance of early investment, in essence, cannot be overemphasized. It is an avenue to economic development, hard work, and stability. Using time, education, and the wonders of compounding, these investors can establish themselves for a successful future. Early intervention not only improves the possibility of building up wealth but also creates a lifetime behavior of spending sensibly and financial planning.

CHAPTER 2: SETTING THE RIGHT INVESTMENT GOALS

Clarifying Your Financial Objectives

Making and setting definite financial goals is another big step any new investor must know before entering into stock market investing. You have to ensure that your investment strategy is in line with your finances by determining your short-term or long-term goals. The initial action in this would be to look deeply within yourself and what you actually desire to attain in terms of financial numbers. This could be retirement savings, buying a home, paying for education, or other forms of wealth building. The various goals will come with their own timelines and risk profiles, and these should define the way you invest.

Start by describing your purpose for investing. This is a precursor to coming up with a roadmap that would be able to work with your life goals. A good example here is that, should your goal be to retire comfortably, then what does that mean to you financially? This may include the calculation of how much money you would require in a year after retirement and factoring in inflation and life expectancy. Equally, when attempting to purchase a house, you must know exactly how much you are expected to pay as a down payment and how soon you expect to buy it.

At this stage, you should be fully aware of what you have to achieve, but the next stage is to make these big aims into actual goals. This is a practice where one breaks big goals into small goals that are easy to achieve. As an illustration, a general objective such as I would like to have 1million to retire on, can be separated into yearly savings goals, investments paid up, and schedules. Not only will this increase the likelihood that the objective may be realized, but it will give a light to walk in.

Another very important thing is to define your investment strategy according to your own risk profile and lifestyle. Each individual has a different risk tolerance, depending on age, income consistency, debts, and comfort level with the movement of the market. The younger investor may take greater risks as he has more time to recover the loss, whereas the older investor may want to act more conservatively to protect his capital.

To help in such alignment, most resources will propose that you use a decision tree or a quiz that will help to define your risk comfort level and investing style. This can aid you in selecting the preferred way ahead, a non-controlling practice to use (which may contain index-based funds or ETFs) or one centered on growth (which may include individual stocks). Also, your goals and strategies should be examined and updated according to the change in your life and financial status.

One more crucial point that must be considered is the avoidance of the FOMO (Fear of Missing Out) and the comparison traps. People often get carried away by the hype in the market or by the success of others, and these are likely the unexpected decisions that make them spend their finances according to situations, rather than according to what they want and what they have planned. Rather, concentrate on what you need in life and what plans are in your best interests. This concentration will assist in gaining trust and will be successful in the long run in your investing adventure.

To recap it all, clarifying your financial goals is related to knowing what you want, how to conceptualize it into action, how your risk makes sense with financial goals and zoning out so that you do not lose focus on your journey because a blaring noisy world wants to interfere with what you plan on doing. It will be a strong basis for your investment choices and will enable you to have purposeful and confident stock market ramblings.

Short-term vs Long-term Goals

When discussing the concept of investing, short-term and long-term goals play a vital role in making the development of the strategy consistent with the financial goals and risk that an individual is willing to take. Each of these ways has its advantages and disadvantages, and understanding well what way to choose or how to combine both, one may greatly influence the success of the investor.

Short-term objectives in investing are normally those that are supposed to be completed within a few months to a few years. These could be to save up for a vacation, a wedding, or a down payment on a car. The main concern under this is liquidity and security; there is a security that the money will be there when it is required. Since there is less time to invest, short-term investments are usually invested in less risky instruments, such as savings accounts, certificates of deposits, or short-term bonds. The point is that risk should be minimized because less time is available to overcome any critical situations inside the market.

Long-term goals, on the other hand, are those goals that are planned several years or even decades into the future. Those may consist of a pension fund, paying for a college education, or developing a large stock of investments. The long-term planning gives the flexibility to tolerate risk because the market gets time to absorb the ups and downs. It is here that investments in stocks, mutual funds, and real estate will be more attractive. In the long run, they tend to experience a relatively better performance on returns, though they were more volatile. Another aspect called the compounding effect is of great importance in long-term investing, where the reinvested profits can earn extra income in the long run.

Whether to pursue short-term or long-term goals is greatly determined by the financial status of a person, their age, and the amount of risk they are willing to take. Young investors would be interested in long-term growth, as it benefits from the compounding effect and the tolerance to overcome the volatility of the markets. On the other hand, older investors or those at the end of the working term might be more interested in shorter-term stability and capital maintenance to have enough liquidity to cater to future needs.

To find an equilibrium between short-term and long-term objectives, one must have a strategic approach, and this approach may include a diversified portfolio. This may involve investing part of the investments in low-risk, sound investments to take care of short-term and exposing the other part to risky but growth-oriented investments to take care of long-term requirements. It is also important to review and adjust portfolios on a regular basis to make them conform to the changing financial objectives and market situations.

Note that the effect of taxes on the returns of the investment must also be taken into account by the investor since the rates of capital gains tax vary at different holding periods. A higher tax is charged on short-term investments, which are investments that are supposed to be retained for a year or less. Knowledge of these intricacies can aid in the optimized investment process and maximize returns post-tax.

In the end, a decision is not mutually exclusive sometimes. An investment portfolio usually integrates both of these depending on the personal situation of the investor and his/her goals. A clear determination of their goals and the timeframes that each one would take can be described before making any decision that can benefit both the present and future interests of the investors.

Risk Tolerance and Personal Comfort

It is imperative to know the risk tolerance level once joining the stock market as an investor. It not only determines the selection of investments, but also the whole strategy, harmonizing with personal comfort and economic objectives. Risk tolerance could be considered as the level of fluctuation in the returns of investments that a person can tolerate. It differs considerably between investors and is highly personal, depending on the financial position, investment objectives, and emotional stamina.

In determining the level of risk, ability and willingness should be looked at insofar as their aspect of risk-taking. Risk-taking capacity is usually associated with personal finances such as income, savings, and investment time horizon. An example would be an early-stage employee who has plenty of years to retirement and has a relatively stable income; his/her risk tolerance is possibly higher than a person who is approaching his/her retirement age and will therefore be more inclined to hold on to capital instead of making aspirational growth.

Risk tolerance, however, is mostly dependent on personal comfort and emotional reaction to market movement. Certain people will panic in case of mild changes in the value of their investments, whereas other people will not be affected by the substantial amount of turbulence. Apprehending this factor includes analyzing oneself and, in some cases, market experience to identify the feeling when an individual makes a gain or loss.

Risk tolerance can be incorporated into investing through tools and strategies used by the investor. One such strategy is diversification, where investments are spread to contain risk across classes of assets. A diversified portfolio could consist of a combination of assets such as stocks, bonds, and other securities, and a balance between the risky and the stable securities. This strategy is used to smooth out the returns over a period, thereby protecting against the possibility of market corrections.

The investors should also consider the time frame of the investment, as it also affects risk tolerance. The longer time difference gives more time to recover the losses in a bad market situation; thus, more risky investments may be considered. On the other hand, the smaller time horizon may require a more conventional strategy, one that is capital retention oriented.

In addition to monetary reasons, investing in accordance with personal values and objectives may increase comfort. As an example, certain investors may prioritize ethical investing by either investing in stocks or funds with which they identify, even at a different risk level. Some may invest in particular areas they have faith in, say technology or renewable energy, and customize their portfolio to what they regard as their interests and beliefs.

Another aspect of being aligned with risk tolerance and comfort is to go through the portfolio and update it on a regular basis. The capacity and desire to be a risk-taker may alter as the conditions of life vary. Regular reviews make the investor review their approach, therefore, being sure that it fits their situation and future expectations.

Finally, the process of finding a balance between the risk tolerance and the individual comfort is a changing process. It involves persistent reflections and modifications in regard to both the outside market situation and internal emotional reactions. With a due appreciation of risk tolerance, investors can make wise decisions based on that and be less stressed out. They are likely to achieve success with their investments from a long-term perspective. This consistency not only encourages the monetary growth but also ensures that the path to the desired destination truly becomes a rewarding experience.

Creating a Personalized Investment Plan

Designing an individual investment portfolio is an important phase that should be taken by any novice investor who wants to venture into the world of the stock market. It starts by clearly comprehending your financial goals, risk tolerance, and period. These aspects underlie the creation of an approach that can fit personal needs and requirements.

The initial move in establishing this type of plan is to describe your financial goals very clearly. Do you have retirement, a child in education, or do you want to make your wealth? The goals can take various approaches. As an example, retirement, which is a long-term goal, may have a more active portfolio strategy that includes higher investment in stocks. In contrast, short-term goals may require a more passive, stable portfolio, where the main constraint is capital preservation.

Then it is very important to determine your risk tolerance. This goes into realizing the amount of risk that you are comfortable taking without having sleepless nights because the market moves up or down. You can find different questionnaires and tools that would allow you to assess the degree of your risk, which can be conservative or even aggressive. An aggressive investor can invest a large percentage of dividend-paying stocks and growth stocks in the portfolio. In contrast, the conservative investor may put the largest percentage of the portfolio in bonds.

Time horizon is also a key determining factor in the shaping of your investment plan. The greater the amount of time you are willing to invest, the greater the degree of risk that you can usually tolerate, since there is a longer available period to recoup losses. On the other hand, a shorter time-horizon may also require a more conservative stance, emphasizing capital preservation, albeit modest growth.

As soon as all these keys are established, you can proceed to creating the real portfolio. The main idea here is diversification, whereby investment objectives are to be diversified among various asset classes in order to reduce risk. This could contain a combination of stocks, bonds, mutual funds, and exchange-traded funds (ETFs). The asset classes respond differently to different market conditions, and proper diversification of the portfolio can move returns more evenly over time.

In addition, you should check your investment plan frequently and update it. Your investment strategy should also change depending on the varying personal situations and market conditions. Periodical reviews enable assessment of re-balancing of your portfolio as it keeps to your objectives. This could include the possibility of selling assets that have grown out of proportion and buying assets that have been underrepresented in your preferred asset allocation.

Lastly, negotiate the cost in your investment scheme. Expenses and fees have the potential to eat away at the returns every year, and this is why low-cost investment vehicles should always be preferred. Index funds and ETFs are popularly suggested due to their low expense ratio and market exposure features, which make them ideal to start with.

To sum up, a personal investment plan can be arranged in the following steps: formulating financial objectives, determining a level of risk, time horizon of the strategy, asset diversification, and the strategy review and modification. These steps will help investors to make a plan that not only fulfills their immediate needs but also keeps up with changes in the future, setting the stage for their financial success in the long term.

Chapter 3: Navigating the Stock Market

Understanding Market Fluctuations

Every novice in the complicated stock market investment world should know how the market moves. The market is an organism and fluctuates between tides and out-tides and always responds or reacts to a myriad of stimuli. Such variations are not arbitrary, and the actions that affect them include a complicated interaction of various forces like economic signs, investor business attitudes, and geopolitics. The understanding of these factors can make new investors take decisive action, instead of being carried along with the usually turbulent market waves.

Economic data is one of the main drivers of market movement. Factors such as the rate of employment, growth rate in GDP, inflation rates, and consumer confidence are some of the indicators that may greatly influence the investor. To take an example, a report on a resounding job creation would imply a healthy economy that can encourage investor sentiment to propel the stock markets upwards. On the other hand, the increased levels of inflation may introduce worries of high interest rates, which then cause the market to go down since the customers expect their interest rates to rise.

Another very important component is investor sentiment. The market is often influenced by emotions and not by logic. This psychological factor may result in such phenomena as bull and bear markets. The bull market is where optimism is felt, and all the investors are keen to purchase investments, thus causing prices to increase. Conversely, a bear market is short of optimism and inclination to sell, and gives way to a decline in prices. Both types of emotional cycles can help a beginner to understand how the market might be overbought or oversold in order to get an opportunity to buy at low levels and sell at high levels.

The market is also subject to fluctuations in terms of geopolitical occurrences. Political instability, issues, or fluctuations in trade or government policies may cause increased volatility. As an illustration, the supply chain can be disrupted in the case of a trade war, thus affecting the corporate profits and the confidence of an investor, hence making the stock prices suffer. On the same note, the alteration of government regulations can help build or hamper the growth of a market due to the kind of change being made and how useful it is likely to be.

In addition, market changes can result from technological advancements and innovations. Those industries that are fast in embracing new technology normally grow where investors come in, and the company's stock rises. On the other hand, industries that are slow in innovation may experience a loss of their value in the market. By following technological trends, it becomes possible to indicate how the market will move in the future, hence giving investors the opportunity to position themselves well.

Global events also determine the market fluctuations. Markets all over the world may be shaken by natural calamities, epidemics, or international wars, which develop uncertainty. Such occurrences may disturb economic activity and consumer behavior, and result in variance in resource allocations, all of which may cause crime in the stock prices.

To those who are new to the market and dealing with fluctuating market forces, the main trick is to become firm in developing an understanding of these fundamental forces. Being informed and having a long-term direction will keep new investors out of the dangers of panic selling when markets fall and euphoric buying when they are rising. They can rather work on constructing a diversified portfolio that evades risk and exploits opportunities in the market.

Summing up, at the beginning of the period spent on the market, its fluctuations can be intimidating; however, they provide important information about the health of the market and its future tendency. Through the knowledge of causes and effects of such fluctuations, a beginner can then make better decisions and develop a long-term base in the stock market. The key tools needed in this voyage are patience, discipline, and a desire to learn always, as these attributes help an investor not only to survive the tempestuous situations of market volatility but also live the best of it.

Bull and Bear Markets

In this eternally changing sphere of the stock market, there exist two predominant issues that tend to attract the minds of investors: bull markets and bear markets. These terminologies, though apparently abstract, in fact explain the current atmosphere of the market, to which the approaches of investors as well as their feelings are directed.

A bull market is described as a period of increase in stock prices, which in most cases is facilitated by optimism and investor confidence and the prospects of further good performance. It is a show of bull charging, more visible proof of the push and aggressive buying power that is characteristic these days. In cases of a bull market, investors are more than willing to enter the market in a rush, often too readily fueled by the fear of losing out on profits. This optimism, although a good thing in the rise of prices, can also produce valuations that are not sustainable, and there should be a degree of caution in order to avoid such an effect.

Conversely, a bear market is a fall in stock prices and can be caused by an economic slowdown, bad news, or general pessimism. You can imagine a bear, lumbering, defensive, the embodiment of the reticent defensiveness of the market at these times. Investors are likely to dump their stocks either to salvage the loss or fear further losses, which in some cases may result in panic selling with a resultant downward trend of decline reinforcing itself. Bear markets can be a very emotional experience with an excessive amount of fear and uncertainty pervading investor moods.

Investors, especially those who are inexperienced, need to understand the psychological as well as practical effects of such way-cycles in the market. Bubble markets may promote high-risk behaviour, like making hasty investments or the overstretching of the already acquired financial power. On the other hand, bear markets may encourage rash asset-sale decisions, in which case people may realize their losses and fail to recover.

To successfully go through these cycles, investors ought to pay attention to having a balanced approach and a long-term vision. During a bull market, one has to remain a realist and not follow each emerging stock, as most of the time, this has yielded poor performance. Investors must, however, concentrate on ensuring that their portfolios are diversified and that they follow their investment plans, irrespective of the market euphoria.

Bear markets need patience and discipline. Instead of panicking, investors are advised to analyze their portfolios, re-evaluate their monetary objectives, and seek opportunities to purchase high-quality stocks that can be underpriced. It is also a moment to reconsider the levels of risk tolerance and see whether the investment pattern fits the personal financial goals.

Both bull and bear markets are schools of learning to develop the dynamics of market factors and approaches of any investor. It is important to identify the symptoms of every stage and realize their consequences so that investors will be able to prevent their main trappings and make things go their way. As the market goes up or down, an effective strategy that is based on research and a strategic plan can help an investor to overcome the euphoria and the hard times in the stock market with more composure and stability.

Reading Stock Charts and Graphs

Stock charts and graphs are critical in investing in the stock market, especially among novices. These charts are like a window to the past data on the performance of a stock, and could provide valuable information that is not expressed by numerical data. As we like to flick through a stock chart, it is not a series of lines and bars, but it is a route of market forces, actions taken by investors, and economic effects, which have been knit together through time.

A stock chart will usually comprise a selection of candlesticks or bars in which price actions are symbolized during a period, e.g., daily, weekly, or monthly. Each candlestick consists of a body and wicks, where the body can be related to the opening and closing prices, and the wick can be measured as high and low prices at that point. This basic illustration enables the investors to determine at a glance and a given moment whether the stock price closed at a better or an even lower price than it was opened initially, which offers an insight into the market trend immediately.

Other than the simple candlestick, the user will observe other forms of technical indicators that are incorporated in the charts. Market indicators such as the moving averages, relative strength index (RSI), and the volume bars serve a very useful purpose in the interpretation of market dynamics. Moving averages are used to smooth price data to see trends over time and thus help an investor tell whether a stock is in a downtrend or an uptrend. The RSI, in its turn, determines how fast and how prices are changing, showing whether they are in overbought or oversold areas.

The bars mostly shown at the bottom of a chart that show the volume of shares traded in a period are called volume bars. A large volume usually confirms the power of a price movement, which implies that the current trend may persist. On the other hand, low liquidity would trigger no serious belief in the market, which would be a victim of possible reversals.

Although these aspects form the spine in the analysis of stock charts, the chart patterns are equally important. Patterns, like heads and shoulders, two tops, or triangles, are visual constructions that predict possible improvements or changes in the market. Awareness of such patterns may provide forecasts on the direction of future prices, thus enabling investors to be in a better position to make sound investing decisions.

The understanding of stock charts is not limited to the appreciation of trends and patterns alone; the study involves the context of occurrences of the movements. Economic news, you know that information which comes out of the capital markets about earnings, geopolitical events, etc, can move the price of stocks dramatically, and so should be taken into account in chart interpretation. As an example, an unexpected surge in volume and price may be explained by a good earnings announcement or a new product.

Furthermore, it is impossible to overestimate the psychological side of reading charts. Charts usually depict the mass psychology of the investors, and market forces are usually ruled by fear and greed. Investors can know about these emotional undercurrents and even know what to expect in terms of market reactions, and then develop an appropriate strategy to follow.

The art of reading stock charts and graphs is, in a way, more of a science than gut feelings. It will need eye-catching details, knowledge of technical indicators, and interpretation of the market situation. This capability is essential to the stock market newcomer who must make sense out of impenetrable information and turn it into useful information. When a person learns to read these visual representations, the capacity to forecast and act in regard to market fluctuations turns out to be a potent weapon in the portfolio of the investor.

Using Market Indicators

Learning how to navigate through the indicators of the market is very important to a person who tries himself in the field of stock market investing. These signs are very important as they act as guides to letting investors know about the shifts in the market so that they can make a good investment. Market indicators are diverse and unique in their determination and use. They may be divided into the leading, lagging, and coincident indicators, which give various views on the market changes.

Those indicators are the leading indicators as they are likely to change before the economy begins to move in a given direction. They can never be underestimated in their ability to forecast the next move and are usually a tool investors rely on to forecast changes in the market. These are stock market returns, building permits, and the money supply. These indicators are not perfect, and they must be applied along with other data to make well-argued decisions.

The lagging indicators, in turn, respond to the changes within the economy and are applied to prove trends that are already taking place. They are necessary to confirm the trends forecasted by leading indicators. These are the unemployment rate, profits of firms, and the cost of labor per unit. They are indicators that enable investors to ensure that a certain trend is sustainable.

Commercially, there are coincident indicators that move more or less around the same time as the economy, giving a real-time view of the economic conditions. These incorporate gauges such as personal payroll, gross domestic product, and retail sales. These indicators are especially helpful in knowing the health of the economy as they enable investors to make their investments by knowing what the economy has to offer at the moment.

Another important instrument is technical indicators, which are commonly applied along with fundamental tools to forecast market direction in the future. These are mathematical computations utilizing previous price, quantity, or open interest data. These are the relative strength index (RSI), the MACD (moving average convergence divergence), and moving averages, among others. Technical indicators are useful for distinguishing tendencies and reversal limit points in the marketplace to give a more detailed picture of market dynamics.

The market mood can be analyzed using the indicators of market sentiment (Fear and Greed Index or Volatility Index (VIX)). The indicators are important in defining the psychological background to the movements in the market. A great deal of fear may be a good sign of a possible buying opportunity, whereas too much greed may be a good sign that there will be a market correction.

Other important factors are the economic indicators that shape the market dynamics, like the interest rates, the inflation rates, and the fiscal policies. The rate of interest, for example, may affect investors' behavior regarding the cost of borrowing. The inflation rates influence the purchasing power, and consumer behavior may change, which affects the stock prices.

To a novice, these indicators might appear overwhelming to master. Nevertheless, having several crucial signs to begin with and increasing their knowledge step by step, investors may create the whole world of instruments, allowing them to survive in the stock market jungle. The main point is that one should not use only one of the indicators. The comprehensive activity that involves different indicators will present a better image of the market and will allow for better decisions.

Trading in investments with the indicators present in the market entails learning and adapting. They should also change the indicators used as the market situations change. By keeping informed and becoming flexible, investors can improve their capacity to predict the changes experienced in the market and refine their investment plans.

CHAPTER 4: CHOOSING YOUR INVESTMENT PATH

Active vs Passive Investing

When it comes to investing in the stock market, it is important to know the main streams of investing strategies, namely, active and passive ones. These two approaches are different, but the common factor is that they are aimed at raising maximum returns. Still, the difference between the two approaches lies in the methodology, risk, and effort applied.

Active investing is termed as being hands-on. Fund managers or investors pick securities actively and monitor the portfolio, and actively change these securities or adjust the portfolio to benefit from market movements. Such an approach is based on the fact that an individual is able to beat the market due to skillful analysis and timing. Real-time investors encompass a big deal of research, market projections, and timing of the trades. This way of conducting business would demand profound knowledge of market forces, business performance, and economic trends. It aims to take advantage of the short-term price change and to purchase or sell an asset that has been evaluated as having intrinsic worth when compared with the market price.

Higher returns may be considered one of the primary benefits of active investing. Through more active portfolio management, investors can take advantage of inefficiencies and trends within the markets that an active portfolio philosophy might not detect. What is more, active investing gives an opportunity to be freer in adapting to market conditions and changing them according to new information, encouraging investors to respond to the updated information or economic change in a fast manner. However, with this possibility of greater returns, greater risk and volatility are witnessed. Active management: Active management may incur costs in the form of frequent transaction costs and management costs, which may also reduce returns in the long term. Moreover, being less predictable, active investing depends considerably on the competency and proficiency of the investor or the fund manager.

Passive investing, on the other hand, is more laid back. The portfolio-building approach would entail building or creating a portfolio that would replicate the performance of a certain index, like the S&P 500. The passive investors are of the opinion that the markets are efficient, meaning that they have the perception that it is hard to beat the market over a long period. Passive investors are people who have invested in index funds or exchange-traded funds (ETFs) to ensure that they obtain returns that equal the market or reduce work in managing the fund.

The principal benefits of passive investing are its low cost and ease of use. The less money that goes to pay transaction costs and management fees, the greater the amount of money the investor can have in the investment market, which might result in more net returns in the long term. Passive investing is also less volatile and risky as it does not run into the trap of market timing. Such a strategy will demand less time and experience and therefore will be available to more investors, including novices. The trade-off, however, is that the passively managed investors are basically settling for the average returns in the market and potentially risk losing the chance to outperform the market as compared to the bear markets.

In the end, the preference towards passive and active investment will be based on the investment objective, the level of risk that one can take, and the amount of time and effort that one can devote to managing the investment. Even the most aggressive investors might hybridize these two approaches, such that passive investments constitute a foothold that provides stability, and active investments are intended to improve performance. Learning about the peculiarities of each style helps investors make educated choices that correspond to their financial demands.

Growth vs Income Investments

Growth investments and income investments can be considered as the two major approaches that can be used in stock market investing and can be of main interest to new and experienced investors. The strategies have different ways of attaining financial objectives, which suit different investors ' tastes, risk tolerance, and long-term goals.

Capital appreciation is the main target of growth investments. Investors engaging in this strategy normally look at companies with high potential for increasing their earnings, whereby they may reinvest any interests earned back into the company, which leads to more growth than paying shareholders in the form of dividends. The business consists of companies that are often on the edge of innovation, and they are in dynamic industries of technology, biotechnology, or emerging markets. Investments in growth businesses are alluring in the sense that such investments may yield high returns since the value of the business appreciates with time. However, this upside of enjoying greater rewards also comes with a similar amount of risk, as these companies could be more unpredictable and prone to changes in the market.

On the contrary, the emphasis of income investments is to produce a consistent stream of income in the form of dividends or interest payments. This approach is attractive to those investors who desire consistent payments, usually to be retired or supplement other sources of income. Income-based portfolios normally entail dividend-paying stock, bonds, or other interest-bearing assets. The characteristic of such investments is that they are usually more stable and have a relatively small risk as compared to growth stocks. The companies belonging to this group are typically larger, mature companies whose cash flow is predictable, utilities or consumer staple companies, which tend to earn profits and pay back a share of such profits to investors in the form of dividends.

The difference between growth investment and income investment depends on a number of factors, such as the financial objectives of the investor, the time frame any investor has on their hands, and the risk orientation of the investor. Growth assets tend to suit a longer-term investor who is ready to operate with a higher risk level in order to enjoy chances of increased capital gains. This strategy would attract younger investors as they have a considerable time horizon and can withstand market fluctuations and the advantages of compound returns over time.

In contrast, income investments might suit the people who are close to retirement or wish to retain the capital and gain a stable income. It is a more conservative strategy that deals with the preservation of wealth and the stability of its income. Income investors prefer to invest in income investments because they are focused on cash flow and are willing to forego growth to feel more financially secure without putting their capital at the above-average risk that comes with growth stocks.

In the end, the growth/income investment conflict is not a mutually exclusive decision. A mix of both strategies has value to many investors who prefer to have a diversified portfolio. It is through growth and income investments that one can ensure that their portfolio best suits his or her personal financial goals, risk preferences, and age to maximize the investment experience based on growth potential and the stability of the income. This is a moderate position that enables investors to enjoy the advantages of both methods and gives an ideal combination of capital growth and income growth. This aspect fosters investment goals in the long run.

Diversification Strategies

An investment portfolio should include diversification, which is the most important guideline to control risk and maximize returns. The diversification of investments will ensure that the volatility is smoothed by protecting the investor against the negative effects of the poor performance of any particular investment through pooling much capital into a wide range of investments in different asset classes, sectors, and across geographies.

The ability to diversify is based on the age-old wisdom that states, Do not put all your eggs in one basket. This is an easy analogy for determining the necessity of diversifying investments in order to reduce exposure. When investments are concentrated in a single area, like a stock or a particular sector, the overall performance of the portfolio will be very sensitive to the performance of the particular investment. On the contrary, diversification will enable other investments to have a chance of balancing any possible loss in case one of the investments falls short.

The advantages of diversification are especially important to new investors. It serves as a buffer to the unpredictability of the stock market, which is prone to sudden drops in individual stocks owing to unforeseen events. Through a diversified selection of investments ranging across different industries, including technology, healthcare, and consumable goods, as well as several asset classes, including bonds and foreign stocks, investors are able to secure their portfolios against dramatic declines in any one given field.

Stocks are not the only way of diversification. It covers a mix of different asset classes, such as bonds, real estate, commodities, and cash equivalents. The different asset classes have varying responses to economic occurrences; hence, they have a stabilizing influence on the portfolio. As an example, when stock markets are volatile, the bond could be stable since they are not strongly tied to economic swings most of the time. Likewise, global diversification may be used to cushion against recession at the home front by taking advantage of other areas that are growing.

Or a good example of what would be an effective diversification could be a combination of technology stocks with a healthcare and a consumer staples stock, with a bond

ETF providing stability, and a global stock, such as an international ETF, to capture the international growth trends. Such a portfolio may show a more consistent future outcome (a lower value) of growth and risk reduction.

However, diversification also carries pitfalls and industry myths that all investors need to avoid. False diversification is one of these traps, which takes place when investors tend to think that they are diversified because they hold numerous stocks. In the event that all these stocks are in the same industry, like technology, the portfolio may still be under threat if the said industry suffers a depression. The real diversification is the investment category, which is investing in separate, slow areas, parts, and areas.

The other risk consideration includes the over-concentration risk, whereby excessive concentration in a certain asset or a sector can result in tremendous losses in case the area does not perform well. Investors should review their portfolios and rebalance regularly in order to keep their portfolios well diversified.

In a nutshell, diversification is a survival strategy that mitigates risk and increases the chances of returns through spreading investments across a wide range of opportunities. It is a pillar of effective investing, especially for a less experienced investor who might be more vulnerable to the movement of the market. Through the knowledge and applications of effective diversification techniques, investors are able to construct strong portfolios that are not affected by the ups and downs in the economy to ensure sustainable growth, which is steadier.

Building a Balanced Portfolio

The development of an effective investment portfolio can be compared to building a management team, where each member has a fundamental role to play in the realization of a similar result. The main objective has been to combine various asset classes not only to maximize returns but also to provide a hedge against loss in case of a mismatch. This is balanced through diversification, which is the idea of diversifying the investment portfolio through different types of financial instruments, sectors, or other categories so that one does not become exposed to a particular asset or risk.

Imagine a portfolio as a pie, and each slice will be a different type of asset. The traditional assets are stocks, bonds, and cash, though lately portfolios might consist of real estate and commodities as well as foreign investments. All the categories exhibit differing behaviors in different market conditions, and a combination of them can provide stabilization to the volatility of any individual investments.

Stocks are the main constituent of most portfolios as they can give high returns. They sell shares in firms and, therefore, receive a share in later profits. They are, on the other hand, riskier, because they can change in price drastically. Bonds, in their turn, are usually safer. They make fixed payments on interest and are not volatile, and therefore act as a stabilizing portfolio. Cash, despite having the lowest return, is essential for liquidity, whereby an investor is able to take up opportunities in the market or to foot unforeseen costs without being forced to dispose of other investments at a loss.

Portfolio balancing is an art that consists of the distribution of the resources within a portfolio according to their financial objectives, risk tolerance, and the investment period. Younger investors may choose to have a growth-oriented portfolio in terms of holding more stocks, as they have plenty of time. People close to retirement would like to have a defensive combination, which focuses on the protection of capital.

A favourable programme of preserving this balance is rebalancing, which implies realigning the portfolio with the initial allocation. This is usually the nature of the process by selling those assets that perform well and purchasing more of the less performers, as it is a disciplined practice which, in the long run, may work out and increase returns on the thesis of buying low and selling high.

Besides, diversity is also valuable within asset classes. This refers to diversification in the stock market, whereby investments are made in various industries and geographical locations. With bonds, it will consist of government bonds, municipal bonds, and corporate bonds in different maturities and credit quality.

A diversified portfolio is more feasible than ever before with the creation of modern tools and platforms that help to build and maintain one. Diversification especially comes when the exposure to a variety of assets is provided; this is done through exchange-traded funds (ETFs) and mutual funds, in which the participation of even small-scale investors would be aided. Such funds are usually set up to follow certain indices, creating a pre-packaged diversified investment.

Finally, a balanced portfolio is not a set-it-and-forget-it project that needs to be reviewed periodically and revised as the market fluctuates and life changes. Investors have to be familiar with the current information and be dynamic enough to adjust to it and keep the chosen balance. Such actions enable them to safeguard their investments and be in a suitable position to exploit new opportunities, hence making significant progress towards their financial goals.

CHAPTER 5: GETTING STARTED WITH STOCK TRADING

Opening a Brokerage Account

To embark on the venture into the stock market investing, it is best to open a stable entry point: a brokerage account. It now appears as the first step and may look big and scary, but this is the main stone of your investing future. To facilitate this process, it is necessary to know the peculiarities of opening a brokerage account.

The first step involved in the work is choosing a brokerage firm that suits your preferences and investment objectives. This choice is crucial since each of the lending companies has varying services, charges, and tools. In the process of selection, pay attention to the trading fees, the size of the minimum investment, the convenience of usage, customer support, and learning material. Others are focused on beginners who can use them easily and have access to ready educational resources. Others are oriented to more experienced traders who have access to sophisticated trading features.

After you decide on which brokerage you are going to use, the second step is to register or open an account. This normally starts with an online application, in which you will give your details such as name, address, social security number, and employment. Such data is not only necessary as the records of the brokerage to be, but also as the regulation of monetary transactions needs to be in line with the Know Your Customer (KYC) rule: this rule assists in fraud prevention; in such a way, secure and legal investment is provided.

In the procedure, you will be required to select the type of account you are planning to open. The alternatives normally have individual accounts, joint accounts, or retirement accounts such as IRAs. All the types of accounts are used differently and provide different benefits; hence, it is desirable to choose one according to your financial objectives. As an example, a retirement account may have tax benefits, and a joint account may work better for a shared investment account.

Once you have placed your application, the brokerage will match your identity and details. In this verification, other documents, such as a copy of your driver's license or utility bill, can be given to ascertain your location. Although this may appear to be tedious, it is important to secure and make sure that your account is safe.

After you have had your account approved, the second step is to invest in it. Depositing Methods Brokerages usually provide several ways to send funds, such as connecting your bank account so it can be directly transferred, sending a wire transfer, or even mailing checks to the company. The most important thing is to begin comfortably, depending on the status and investment plan you want to follow. It has become easier to start with a low amount of money to deposit, which is the case in many brokerages today, enabling you to start small and add to your portfolio in the long run.

Since your account has been activated, it is time to discover the capabilities of the platform. Become acquainted with the modules offered, e.g., research materials, educational articles, and trading demonstrations, that might turn out to be invaluable to a novice. Most of the platforms also have mobile applications, so that you can take care of your investments even when you are not on the screen, and thus, it is even more convenient and a part of the routine.

Simply, to invest in the stock market, it will be necessary to open a brokerage account. You have taken a big step toward your investment when you choose the correct platform, learn how the application works, and acquire knowledge on the tools offered there. This is an easy first step, which will open the book of opportunities in the way of the stock market, flying you on the route to financial stability and prosperity.

First Steps in Buying Stocks

When a person visits the stock market to invest in stock market securities, it appears like they are in a maze of options and processes that are new to them. Nonetheless, this process can be simplified by learning the basic steps one has to take to buy stocks and enabling new entrants to be in a stronger position to make sound decisions. Before you do this, the initial task is to find a brokerage platform that is in line with your investment orientations and your experience. The decision you make here will form the base of your investment activities since the various brokerages have different fee structures, types of user interfaces, and resources based on whether one is a novice or a more experienced trader.

After deciding on the brokerage, the second step would be opening a brokerage account. The process has become extremely simplified by the introduction of online services, which enable individuals to establish their accounts from the comforts of their residential homes. In this step, it is important to put appropriate personal details such as your social security number and job details in order to satisfy the needs of regulations and the security of the account.

The next thing is to fund your newly opened brokerage account. It is possible with different mechanisms, like a connection with a bank account, wire transfer, or a mobile check deposit. There are always more suggestions for new investors to begin with a small investment, which can be as minimal as 100 dollars, since in this way, one will take less risk and have some practical experience. The idea of fractional shares may also be beneficial as it would enable the investor to get a share of the high-value stock without parting with as much money.

Having deposited some money into your account, it is only logical to make your first stock order. This entails determining which form of order is closest to your investment plan, either a market order, the purchase of the stock at its current price, or a limit order whereby you offer to buy the stock at a specific price of your choice. It is vital to have an idea of those types of orders as they determine how your trades are executed and how they are priced.

Before you finally take that step to buy a stock, you must do enough research about the investment you intend to make. This is a study of the company fundamentals, market situation, and other pertinent financial measures. Free services such as Yahoo Finance or Google Finance can give great inspiration as to the performance of the stock and the conditions of the market, and they can assist you in making better decisions.

Lastly, do not fall into the most typical traps that novice traders use, like trading on emotions and following what the market says is the hype, and you may have to rue the fact that you have not diversified your portfolio enough. One strategy relates to diversification, whereby investments are made in various classes of assets in order to minimize risk. A diversified portfolio helps you to stabilize the market ups and downs and improve your chances of experiencing constant returns.

With careful and deliberate observances of these first steps, new investors may establish a firm platform on which they may launch into the stock market. This well-organized process not only eases the introduction into the world of investing but also makes you feel confident and in charge of your finances to come.

Understanding Order Types

To trade in the stock market, a person must have an idea of the various order types available to the investor to place a trade. All the types of orders are created with a specific aim and may assist investors in attaining their financial purposes, as they give them control over the process of buying and selling. Being aware of such connotations is important both in reducing risk and maximizing possible gains.

Market order is the simplest form of the order. It is the easiest method to purchase or sell stock because it enables the investor to close a trade at the given price, which is the current price in the market. The main positive aspect of market order is that it is fast; the transaction gets done, and it makes sure that the investor is able to exploit whatever is going on in the marketplace. The negative aspect about this, however, is that the ultimate price of the execution could be unpredictable, particularly in an insecure market. The price may vary between the order placement and execution, and this will result in a poor purchase price.

The other type of order is the limit order. This kind of order enables investors to write what the highest price is that they would be ready to pay at a purchase or the lowest price they will accept during a sale. There are also limit orders that are helpful when a particular price is the target of the investor. The reason is that they guarantee that a trade would only be made when the market touches a particular price set by the investor, giving higher control of the execution price. Nonetheless, the danger is that the order might never fill up in case the market price does not hit the stated price level, and some trade opportunities might be missed.

Stop-loss orders cannot be ignored when managing risk. In this form of order, once the price of a stock reaches a certain price, the order will automatically sell the stock in order to minimize the loss of the investor on a position. Stop-loss orders are meant to be used especially in a volatile market, and they act as a safeguard that could help avert losses. The brokers are also useful to those investors who are unable to watch the market all the time, as they automate the loss-cutting.

One form of the stop-loss is called a stop-limit order. This is a blend of the features of both stop-loss and limit order. Once the stock reaches the stop price, the order will be converted into a limit order with a corresponding limit price, and this trade can only take place at the limit price or higher. This kind of order offers greater control over execution price compared to a stop-loss order, yet there is a danger that if the stock price keeps declining below the limit price, then that order will not be executed.

Trailing stop orders also allow investors to implement them, wherein a trailing stop order would vary automatically with a change in the price of the stock. A trailing stop order establishes the stop price at a predetermined distance (downward) behind a market price with an added amount called a trailing. The stop price moves with the increase in stock price by the amount of trail, and once the stock price declines, expansion of the stop price is not required. This gives the investor the chance to get guaranteed returns at the same time, leaving room to avoid huge losses.

It can be critical in a decision about investment to learn and understand the different types of orders and their applications. All types of orders have specific benefits and drawbacks; any investor needs to choose the one based on their strategy, risk tolerance, and the situation in the market. When one learns how to use such tools, they can manage to deal with the stock market better and become more successful.

Executing Your First Trade

Making your very first trade on the stock market is a major boost to a young investor. It is the process by which theoretical education is crossed over to practice, and where ideas on buying and selling of securities become practical decisions. The first step to this process consists of picking a brokerage platform that meets your investing requirements, based on user interface, fees, and accessible resources. Robinhood, Fidelity, and Webull are some of the platforms popular among newcomers because of their user-friendly interface and quality educational materials.

With a brokerage account established and funded, usually with an initial investment of a minimum $100 to $500, the next question a trader would want to know would be the kind of orders in which he can engage. The most common are market orders and limit orders. A market order carries out a transaction at the current market price, causing the fastest possible transaction; however, it is done at the expense of price control. On the other hand, a limit order will enable you to specify the highest price you are ready to pay for a stock to gain additional control. Still, the disadvantage of this is that the order might not be filled in times when the stock fails to achieve your stated price.

It is important that prior to making your first trade, you do a speedy analysis of the stock or ETF of your choice. Invest in a simplified checklist to determine the fundamentals of the company, including the performance of the sector, the latest news, and simple measures of its financial health, like growth in revenues and earnings. This basic item avoids the most popular trap of investing in hype as opposed to learning the worth of the investment.

When the time to make your trade comes, go to the trading area of your brokerage application or website. In this case, you will put the ticker of the stock you desire to buy, the type, and the number of shares. Confirm everything on the confirmation screen and make sure that the ticker symbol and the amount are proper, and the estimated price fits your budget.

Once the trade is carried out, your order will first be registered as pending before eventually getting processed. When this is done, you will see your new holdings in your portfolio, where you will monitor their performance over time. It is also a good time to learn about post-trade management, which involves setting up alerts on price movements or news updates on shares and making stop-loss orders so as to avoid big losses.

At this point, it is important not to make rookie mistakes. The most common mistakes when purchasing the ticker symbol are not the correct one, or not completely understanding the margin requirements, and being hit with unknown extra costs. Please get to know about any transaction fees related to trading because they can affect returns on your investments.

And last, think about the first experience in trading. Note down the feelings and thoughts as they appear along the way. This introspection is simply priceless because it assists one in developing a master of his mind, which is very important in the long-term success of investing. You can practice on your strategies so that your initial trade is only the first step in a successful investing process, because, having gotten to know how trade works and how it makes its participants feel, you can always improve your strategies.

Chapter 6: Analyzing Stocks and Companies

Reading Financial Statements

The balance sheet is a reflection of the momentary financial position of a company, what it owns, and what it owes. When investing as a novice, one must familiarize oneself with this document to make informed investment decisions. The balance sheet has two categories, i.e., assets and liabilities. Assets are listed as what the company possesses (cash, inventory, and property), and liabilities are what the company owes (loans and accounts payable). The ledger balance between the assets and the liabilities is the equity, which shows the worth of the company.

In the case of a financial statement, there are more important numbers that beginners should take cognizance of. These are revenue, profit, debt, and the amount of cash. Revenue shows the amount of money the firm earns in relation to the business it carries out, which is vital in evaluating the capacity of the company to make sales. Profit, also known as net income, is the revenue remaining after deducting all expenses. This figure plays a major role in ascertaining the profitability of the company.

Another important measure is debt, which helps to know how much money is owed by the company. The ratio of debt to cash is also a red flag since it might imply that the company is financially unstable. Conversely, a company that has been recording a steady increase in profits could be perceived as a green flag to possible investment. The amount of cash available is important since it reflects the amount of liquidity of the company, that is, whether the company is capable of paying short-term liabilities.

Becoming familiar with some of the popular valuation measures, such as the price earnings ratio (P/E) ratio and dividend yield, will also give beginners power in the investment process. Another useful method that can be utilized to determine the value of a stock as over- or under-valued is the P/E ratio, which is the ratio between the current share price and earnings per share of a company. A ratio of below 15 may show undervaluation, whereas a ratio greater than 30 may show growth pricing. In the same way, the dividend yield, which is a percentage, is also the yearly return on investment by dividends only. As a novice, investors usually aspire for a yield that ranges between 2 and 5 percent.

Screenshots of real financial statements with comments by Yahoo Finance or Morningstar, etc., can be priceless. These graphic aids allow determining the place where the most important numbers can be found and how to understand them quickly. As an example, an analysis of the P/E ratios of companies such as Apple and Ford can reveal the total market expectations, as well as the differences in valuations.

In addition, there is also a need to know about the myths surrounding these metrics. One of the measures, such as the P/E ratio, is not always the best to take since a low one may be a sign of a troubled company. In the same manner, a high dividend yield may not qualify as the safest, as it may indicate an increased risk.

New investors should inspect the red flags and green lights checklist to identify reliable and risky stocks. Signs may consist of a drop in earnings, excessive balance sheet loads, and unstable management. On the contrary, green lights might represent steady growing profits and high cash reserves. These signals can be explained more practically and vividly in case studies comparing successful examples of companies such as Coca-Cola and those that are struggling in the retail business.

Stock research can be simplified by using free and easy-to-access research. These sites offer the needed information without having to subscribe, and therefore, one can start as a beginner. Step-by-step pictures annotated may teach people how to seek and analyse financial information so that users are comfortable navigating the waters in the stock market investment.

Evaluating Stock Performance

Knowing how to assess the level of stocks is vital to any investor, but highly important to the new ones. It is the process when different financial measures and instruments are reviewed that gives us an idea of the health of a company and whether it is capable of providing some returns. With the understanding of these concepts, an investor will be able to make a calculated decision and avoid some of the pitfalls that could result in an investor losing a lot of money.

When learning how to assess stock performance, the best way to start would be to get acquainted with basic financial reports: the cash flow statement, the balance sheet, and the income statement. All these documents provide a glimpse of various features of the financial health of a company. The income statement indicates the profitability of the company in a given time frame and shows the revenue, expenses, and net income. A balance sheet is a measure taken at any one time to show what a company owns (assets) and owes (liabilities), and it emphasizes the equity of the shareholders. In the meantime, the cash flow statement monitors the cash flows, showing the level of efficiency of the operational processes and financial flexibility of the firm.

These statements turn into important financial figures that are utilized in the consideration of stocks. An example of such a widely used ratio would be the Price-to-Earnings (P/E) ratio, which compares the current price of the share to the earnings per share of a company. It assists investors in deciding whether a share price beats or undercodes the profits of the share. The low P/E may indicate a stock that is undervalued, and a high P/E may indicate an overvalued stock, or due to the projection of growth. It should be noted, however, that the consideration of industry standards and the growth opportunities of the company should be taken into account when using this ratio.

The other key ratio is the dividend yield, which shows the amount that the companies will give in terms of dividends on a yearly basis, divided by the price of the stock. This measure can be of great help to those investors who are interested in income and who use dividends as a form of income. A great dividend yield may be appealing, but it will also indicate possible risks a company is experiencing if the dividend yield is significantly higher than the industry average, which implies that the company may not be able to sustain the dividend coverage.

Stock performance also depends much on the levels of debt. To realize the indebtedness of the company, investors ought to look at the debt-to-equity ratio. A high ratio may mean that a company has a lot of dependency on debt funds to run the business, and in case of interest rate fluctuation, it is a risk, or when the company does not have any money, then it is a risk.

Besides these parameters, investors need to know the qualitative parameters, such as competition level, quality of management, and market conditions of a company. All these can greatly affect the performance of a company, hence the stock price.

These data points can be collected and interpreted with the help of such instruments as Yahoo Finance or Morningstar. On these websites, even novice users have the opportunity to read financial reports, primary indicators, and companies' industry comparisons. Through these resources, investors are able to gain an in-depth perception of the performance of a business and are in a better position to make competent investment decisions.

Stock performance is finally a matter of using quantitative research combined with qualitative research to provide a complete image of the potential of a company. The more investors become skilled and adept at reading such signals, the more they will be able to navigate the stock market because of greater confidence and precision in creating their investment plans, depending on how they want to arrive at their financial objectives.

Using Ratios and Metrics

In real life, when you want to invest in the stock market, the ratios and measures are very important to be well-known and taken advantage of when you are a first-time investor. These are the compasses that help investors navigate the tricky financial world and assist in assessing the worth and potential of various stocks. The most important ratios and metrics, on the basis of which this analysis is carried out, are at the center of this analysis, and they help to understand the financial stability and market share of the company.

The price-earnings ratio, commonly abbreviated as P/E ratio, is one of the most basic measures of valuation. It is indicated by the relationship between a company's share price and its earnings per share. The ratio can be used as a gauge to determine whether a stock is overvalued or undervalued when compared to its earnings. A low P/E could be an indicator of an undervaluation of a stock, and could present an opportunity to purchase it. Still, a higher P/E may be indicative of an overvaluation of a stock, and as such, it may be uncertain of its attractiveness to investors with a view to its valuation. However, in any case, investors must pay attention to the P/E ratio from the perspective of industry averages since various industries often have distinct standard P/E ratios.

Dividend yield is another important value that indicates how much the company pays to every investor as an annual dividend in relation to the price of the stock. The metric is especially pertinent to those investors who are interested in income, and it signals the income earned against dividends. It is also good to have a high dividend yield as it would promise constant income streams, but one has to look at the sustainability of the dividends by looking at the payout ratio of the company and cash flow.

Another critical ratio, called the debt-to-equity ratio, shows the percentage of company funding provided by debt as opposed to equity. The high ratio of debt-to-equity may indicate possible financial instability, indicating that a particular company depends on borrowing too much, and this may be a danger, particularly in case the market is volatile. On the other hand, a lower ratio could presuppose another situation, a more conservative financial structure, less dependence on borrowed finances, and hence more risk-free.

Also, the knowledge of Return on Equity (ROE) would be critical because it determines the profitability of a company by displaying how much money a company earns in terms of the amounts invested by shareholders. A high ROE implies a better usage of equity capital, and thus, such companies will be of potential interest to investors who want to see good management performance.

These ratios are very useful, but they need to be examined with particular care and in connection with one another. Using only a single measurement may give improper conclusions. An overall vision should be the goal of an investor, addressing a set of metrics as a whole that will create an image of the financial state of a company and its investment opportunities.

In addition to that, the limitations of these metrics should be noted. These ratios can be affected by the market situation, the economic environment, and the company-specific forces of the company, and such a situation requires a dynamic and flexible approach to the interpretation of these ratios. When combined with a wider scope of analysis, all these metrics help investors to make a more sensible decision, minimizing the risks and increasing their chances of succeeding in the stock market.

To the newcomers, learning the ropes of applying these ratios and measures is one step closer to becoming a self-confident and capable investor. Learning how to measure and understand these financial figures will help the investor to negotiate the intricacies of the stock market in general and end up making smarter and wiser investments as a result.

Researching Industry Trends

In order to survive in the stock market, industry trends are very important to any prospective investor. The stock market is huge, and there are many sectors, and a number of factors, such as technological advances or geopolitical events, influence each sector. Therefore, it may give invaluable information to help you be aware of the trends in these industries so as to have a clue on what to invest in.

An industry trend can be defined as the overall drift or shift that a specific sector is taking as a response to the behavior of both the different companies in the sector and the external factors, like changing rules or consumer perspective. As an example, the emergence and development of renewable energy sources have played a considerable role in the energy industry, driving people to abandon the usage of traditional fossil fuels and instead incorporate more environmentally friendly sources. Early identification of such trends enables informed choices by investors and the positioning of their portfolio in advance to take advantage of emerging growth.

A successful attempt to study trends in the industry can be carried out with reference to financial news and reports. Such sources of financial news, like Bloomberg or Reuters, have the latest news on the market and analyses by professional economists. Such resources can point out the upcoming trends, give insight into market sentiments, and reveal forecasts by industry specialists. Also, an annual report of the top firms in an industry may provide a lot of information, such as strategic plans of the industry, position of the market, and challenges that the industry expects in the coming year, which is important in realizing the path of the industry.

The other way is to track industry-related indicators and measures. To take one example, in the technology patent sector, a monitor on innovation indexes, or even patents registered, can give an inkling into the theme of technology development. In much the same vein, in the health care industry, following appropriate approvals from regulatory agencies such as the FDA can be an indication of changes to occur in the market area. Such signals can be used to gain an advantage when it comes to predicting the possible change that is about to occur in the market forces.

It can also be useful to read about the industry by attending online or real-life conferences and seminars. These gather commercials and experts in the industry, and they engage in discussions on the latest trends, industry problems, and projections. The personal experience obtained during networking with other professionals at such events will give people a first-hand experience and a better understanding of the industry dynamics.

The traditional way to follow industry trends is to use technology, online platforms, and tools, which may help streamline. Such tools as Google Trends may show the popularity of the search phrases concerning certain industries, which signifies the increased customer interest or concern. Similarly, social media sources and activities such as forums can be used to give real-time feedback and evaluation on the mood of the industry, to give a bottom-up view of what happens in the industry.

Lastly, when performing a trend analysis, it is necessary to be critical in thinking. Not all the trends are lasting and are a sign of long-term growth. Some can be short-term or are fuelled by market frenzy. That is why it is necessary to check what the driving force behind a trend is and what effect it might have on the industry overall. This requires analyzing previous data, comparing it to the present changes, and observing whether the pattern has been consistent with larger-scale measures in the economy or society.

To conclude, the topic of researching industry trends can be presented as a complex process of information search and collection utilizing different resources, critical thought, and thinking of strategies. With knowledge and the ability to predict these trends, a person can make better choices in the stock market world and make strategic and smart investments that can supplement their financial needs.

CHAPTER 7: RISK MANAGEMENT AND MITIGATION

Identifying Potential Risks

When it comes to stock market investing, one should learn about the possible risks for a beginner. The world of investment is chock-full of uncertainties, and each action may carry with it enormous monetary consequences. A new person has to work with this sticky ground and be very careful about the type of risks that affect the results of an investment.

Market volatility is one of the greatest risks in stock market investing. Economic signals, geopolitical factors, and market psychology may cause a wild variation in stock quotes. This volatility is scary, particularly to those who are new to the game, as they may not have faced this volatility before. It is important to appreciate that volatility is a characteristic of the stock market. One should not panic and be driven by the immediate market fluctuations to make long-lasting decisions in investment strategies.

The other major threat is the insufficient diversification. One of the errors that most new investors make is to place all the eggs in a basket by tipping too much on one stock or industry. This tendency of excessive focus is harmful in the case that the stock or sector in question does not perform well. This risk can be reduced through diversification by taking investments in different sectors and different asset classes. It makes it more resistant to loss in a single sector and offers greater stability in the financial portfolio.

Another factor to be reckoned with is the financial risk. This entails the monetary well-being of businesses that one invests in. A firm having a lot of debt or experiencing falling revenues is at a high risk of performing poorly or even going bankrupt. Any beginner ought to learn how to read financial statements because it will help him or her show the feasibility and stability of any potential investment. Reports on these major financial figures, like revenue, profit margins, and level of debt, may give one the information on the financial stability of a business firm.

The other danger to watch out for is emotional investing. The stock market may cause an excitement that ranges between the excitement of a bull market and the depression of a bear market. Behind these feelings lies low impulse control, and they may cause impulsive actions like investing in a stock under the influence of fear of missing out (FOMO) or panicking in a crash and selling off. Emotional investing has been known to result in bad decisions, which can damage long-term financial goals. The emotional effect of these decisions can be reduced by developing discipline and adhering to a properly thought-out plan of investing.

Other aspects of investing in the stock market include regulatory and geopolitical risks. Alterations in government policies, regulations, or international relations may have a significant impact on markets and certain industries. For example, the introduction of new rules in the technology sector or trade tension between some of the leading economies can change the value of the stock substantially. Conducting research on events taking place around the world and their likely effects on investment is essential in controlling these risks.

Finally, novices have to watch out for speculative risks. It entails making investments in risky stocks with the expectation of receiving a great return. Although such investments may be rewarding, they do face a risk of immense losses. Such high-risk investments need to be balanced with more reliable and stable investments in order to have a balanced portfolio.

Through appreciating these risks and their possibilities of occurrence, one becomes aware of what to be wary of when venturing into investing in the stock market. To develop strength and success in an investment portfolio, it is important to plan investments with more knowledge of the risks that are bound to be faced.

Using Stop-Loss Orders

Risk management is the most important aspect in the maze, and that is stock market investing. The stop-loss order is one of the most important measures that an investor can use to ascertain the maximum amount of loss that he/she is to incur by quoting an amount at which a certain stock will be sold. This is a safety instrument because the investments are cushioned against a severe dip without having to be monitored all the time.

A stop-loss order is a simple concept. This is done because the investors set a price at which their stock will be automatically sold if it reaches that price point. It is especially advantageous in unstable markets, in which prices are subject to extremely rapid changes. Setting up an a priori sell point also helps investors avoid making emotional choices of selling their stocks in a panic or holding them too long, waiting for them to take off.

Consider that you bought a stock at 100 and you thought it would go up. Nevertheless, you establish the stop-loss order at the price of $90 to protect against the unexpected price drops. When the stock price falls to 90 dollars, a sale is triggered by a stop-loss order, resulting in a 10% loss of investment. This approach not only preserves your assets, but it also develops discipline with a set risk management protocol.

Many trading platforms enable a trader to set up a stop-loss order easily. Normally, investors have the freedom to place their stop-loss directly with their stockbroker's account. The stop-loss orders are usually set on many platforms with a simple interface, and a stop-loss order can be taken by typing the amount they want to stop being priced, and it can be easily incorporated into your trading strategy.

Nevertheless, although stop-loss orders are a potent measure, it does not mean that there are no difficulties associated with them. Another typical trap is being too tight with the stop-loss, so that it will be triggered by standard market movements, which can be described as the death by a thousand cuts. On the other hand, making it too loose may not ensure good degrees of protection against large falls. Consequently, selecting the proper stop-loss point follows the aspect of safeguarding investments and having some space to let the stock naturally.

Besides the mechanical ones, the psychological effects of using stop-loss orders also cannot be overestimated. Automated selling decisions also help investors prevent the stressful and emotional distress that is usually followed by watching the investments crumble. This automation will avoid irrational decisions made in fear or greed and create a more consistent and logical way of investing.

True life anecdotes also prove the worth of stop loss orders. For example, an investor who incurred a 40 percent loss when he was not using a stop-loss order portrays the operational value of such an instrument. On the other hand, instances of missed potential because of failure to use stop-loss orders have been used as a warning to the investor about the usefulness of the given technique in his/her plan.

Finally, the use of stop-loss orders should not be viewed as a silver bullet because every person can make this model fit his or her needs and approach to risk and investing. An investor can maximize his or her risk management by learning and using stop-loss orders properly, and so preserve the investment portfolio.

Hedging Strategies

Hedging is an important aspect in stock investment whereby investors engage in countering risks, such as potential risks that might be involved in stock market investments. It acts as a safeguard strategy, similar to insurance coverage, which counters any adverse market trends. Hedging is all about ensuring that an investment portfolio is balanced by the involvement of a financial instrument or by taking measures in the market to offset the losses a portfolio may encounter.

Options form one of the most popular hedging strategies. Options are the derivatives of a financial nature that provide investors with the privilege, but not the duty, to either buy or sell a security at a particular price during a limited period. An example is that by buying the put options, an investor is able to sell the stocks at predetermined prices, and this is useful when the market drops below the set price. This will be a useful way of limiting the amount of potential losses while still giving treatment to any upward price fluctuations.

Future contracts are another common method of hedging. Such contracts bind the parties to exchange an asset at some future point at a price that has been agreed on to date. Investors commonly utilize futures to hedge against increases and/or reductions in the prices of commodities or other securities. By fixing the prices, the businesses and investors are able to stabilize their financial planning with respect to the market volatility.

Hedging strategies are also based on diversification. This helps investors to diversify their investments by investing in different asset classes, investment sectors, or geographies so that a downturn in just one single investment does not affect their overall portfolio very much. This strategy will help make sure that some of the investments fail to perform well, but at the same time, some of them will grow optimally, offsetting the rest in terms of profits.

Inverse exchange-traded funds (ETFs) are another technique of hedging. These funds are created to reverse the same direction of the index they follow, and they give returns during market falls. These instruments have special applications when investors expect the market to fall and want to safeguard their investments through protective measures.

Hedging does not come without a price and complications. The application of hedging tools usually implies a deep insight into the financial instruments and market processes. Furthermore, the practice of hedging might also result in the weakening of profits in the event of market movement in the favorable direction, since the protective practices might constrain the area of future profit. Therefore, investors should balance the cost of hedging with the possible gain of risk reduction.

Hedging services are an active form of investing in risk management. The latter requires endless check-ups and revision of strategies to match the dynamics of the market and the objectives of investment. Investors should also be cautious about when to introduce the use of hedges and when to allow them to lapse, depending on the market projections and their risk tolerance.

Finally, hedging choice must be consistent with the investor's whole financial strategy and tolerance to risk. Although hedging can be a relief as it provides some level of security to avert downturns in the market, it is a strategy that should not be overly applied as a standalone tool; we must combine it with other investment tools in order to attain a diversified portfolio. By discovering the right time and manner in which one should hedge, investors will be able to predict the nature of the stock market with more confidence and a sense of security.

Emotional Discipline in Investing

As much as knowing how the market behaves, financial indicators, etc., means in the world of investing, being able to control emotions is paramount. Emotional self-control is the quality of keeping a calm head in the face of the ups and downs of the stock market. This is more than the ability to find out when to sell or when to purchase; it is also about being able to control their emotions to make rational decisions instead of acting impulsively.

The emotional stimuli surrounding investors can be voluminous at best and include the excitement of a raging bull market and the panic that rushes in during an unexpected fall. Failure to control such feelings may result in reckless decisions that kill investment plans. As an example, the fear of missing out (FOMO) at the time of a market boom may cause investors to pay inflated prices, and panic selling when the market falls can render temporarily lost profits irreversible.

In order to develop emotional discipline, it is crucial to develop a succinct investment strategy meant to set up tangible objectives, risk appetite, and timeframes. It is a plan that acts as a guide to an investor and can enable them to keep their goals in mind regardless of the market fluctuations. It can enhance consistency in adhering to long-term goals, instead of being an agent of short-term market variability, by continuously examining and revising this plan.

The other important dimension of emotional discipline is the ability to distinguish between noise and information that can be acted upon. It is full of sensational headlines in the financial media that may cause an emotional response in people. The investors should formulate a model that will aid in determining the news that can be of interest to their portfolio and which are just noise. This is done through a critical analysis of news that affects the foundation of what one has invested in and whether it coincides with the long-term plan.

Emotional discipline in investing can be increased by practicing mindfulness and reflection as well. Investors can detect the patterns and biases in their actions by taking time to reflect on the investment decisions made in the past and the underlying emotions that led to such decisions. Such awareness can bring more intelligent decisions. Journaling market reactions or imagining the future of the investments are some of the ways of focusing and decreasing stress.

Another strategy that we can find to be successful is building a support system. An accountability partner or a community of like-minded investors can give some perspective and help with solving problems caused by emotional decision-making. These networks are able to provide reassurance and a common experience that gives a promise of the need to adhere to the plan.

Last but not least, emotional discipline may also be achieved through automation. It can become less tempting to speculate in the market or to make unstructured trading decisions by implementing automatic investments or rebalancing. Automations allow the investors to look beyond the narrow reality and neglect the problem of emotional trading.

Emotional investing is all about the level of discipline to think in such a way that helps us focus on long-run success instead of immediate satisfaction. There is a need for general planning, awareness, and presence in the market, as well as support from fellow dwellers of the nation, as well as smart automation to overcome the lows and highs of the stock market. It is possible to build on these practices and make the investor capable of rational decision-making, which enhances the overall success of the investment decisions made.

CHAPTER 8: UNDERSTANDING INVESTMENT VEHICLES

Mutual Funds and ETFs

A mutual fund is an investment that pools money raised by several investors to invest in a portfolio of different securities, composed of stocks and bonds, among others. Mutual funds provide an avenue to pool the resources of investors so as to gain access to more facilities in the market, as well as diversifying risks under the care of professional fund managers. Such funds are designed to reach some investment goals that they specify in their prospectus, namely growth, income, or balanced. The investors participating in mutual funds have the opportunity to get the assistance of fund managers who determine the decision to purchase or invest in securities. This management is not free; it is normally charged as annual fees referred to as expense ratios, and this may affect the overall returns of the investment.

On the other hand, Exchange-Traded Funds(ETFs) resemble mutual funds in that they also contain a basket of securities, although they trade on stock exchanges as individual stocks do. It enables investors to trade ETF shares throughout the trading day at the market price, unlike mutual funds, which are only quoted at the end of the trading day. ETFs also tend to be cheaper than conventional mutual funds due to an expense ratio, which is of the essence to investors. A high rate of tax efficiency also characterizes them since normally their structure does not attract much capital gains tax in comparison to the mutual funds.

Both mutual funds and ETFs provide diversification of risks since they reduce the risk of exposure to a particular security by dispersing investments into different funds. This will help cushion the effect of low-performing security on the entire portfolio. Mutual funds and ETFs are very convenient as an entry point into the market, though, in the case of beginners, no specific interest in individual stocks is required.

The investment strategy and personal preference frequently constrain mutual funds and ETFs. One can choose mutual funds for a hands-off approach with professional management and ETFs for the flexibility of trading and low fee costs. Moreover, there are mutual funds, where automatic reinvestment plans can be enabled by some investors, thus bringing returns on returns.

When weighing up these investment vehicles, investors need to consider an investment vehicle approach, expense ratios, minimum investment needs, and management type (active or passive). Active management means that fund managers take a strategy to beat the market, and such funds are usually charged higher fees. Passive management index funds (usually do not overperform the index), aim to duplicate the returns of a certain index and are often cheaper.

Also, there is a need to learn the tax consequences of each of the investment types. Although ETFs tend to be more tax-efficient because they uniquely create and redeem shares, they have the potential for capital gain distribution to investors when compared to mutual funds, where they only have to share the capital gain, even when the investor has not sold his or her shares.

In short, mutual funds and ETFs offer basic instruments for creating a diversified portfolio of investments. They will fulfill various needs of investors, that is, the suggestion of professional management or the malleability of trading on an exchange. As an amateur, it is essential to compare these possible opportunities according to personal financial objectives, tolerance of risk, and investment duration to make competent decisions.

Real Estate Investment Trusts (REITs)

Real Estate Investment Trusts (REITs) present a unique opportunity in the investment environment of the stock market world. Investors who desire to add a real estate exposure to their collections may do so without having to buy real property or even manage it in person. REITs are businesses that buy, manage, or invest in income-generating property in various real estate classes. They enable ordinary investors to share in the revenue that is generated due to ownership of commercial real estate without having to invest, maintain, or finance property themselves.

A REIT is organized in a tax-efficient manner. In order to be a REIT, a company must distribute at least 90 per cent of its yearly taxable income in dividend form to its shareholders. This condition enables REITs not to pay corporate income tax, which may turn out to be a great advantage to the rest of the investments. Subsequently, the investors are capable of a constant flow of income, something that is quite favorable to investors seeking regular cash outflow in their investments.

REITs are divided into three types, namely equity, mortgage, and hybrid REITs. Equity REITs are real estate that is owned and professionally run. They also generate profits mainly by leasing space and receiving rents on the properties they own, which may be office buildings, shopping centers, flat apartments, hotels, and so on. Mortgage REITs, on the contrary, extend credit in the form of mortgage-backed real estate by buying or issuing mortgages and securities backed by mortgages. They earn most of their revenue through the interest charged on the mortgaged loans. Hybrid REITs mix investment roles of REITs, which are equity and mortgage REITs.

The high dividend yield is among the greatest advantages of investing in REITs. REITs usually yield better than other equities because REITs are mandated to pay a huge portion of their income as a dividend. This is why they can be considered attractive to the income-oriented investors who might, in fact, be looking to diversify out of the more conventional kinds of fixed-income assets, such as bonds, because, in a given market environment, bonds may not provide the full returns.

The REIT's investment is also diversifying. Since REITs have a large selection of real estate investments, possession of such investments may offer diversification into varying areas of the real estate market, and identical returns might not be associated with the overall performance of the stock market and bonds. Such diversification has the potential of decreasing the volatility of a portfolio and not only gives a hedge against inflation, due to real estate value and rent growing with inflation, but also makes sense as real estate is a unique investment.

REITs, though, are like any other investment, not without their risks. They face the market risk, interest rate risk, and the risk within the category. An example is an increase in the interest rate, which can hurt the REITs since it raises the cost of borrowing and may cause a fall in the property value. Also, recession may influence rent revenues and tenant occupancy in buildings owned by equity REITs.

Nevertheless, the risks have been offset by competitive total returns delivered by REITs over the long run through high dividend income levels that are stable and long-term capital gains. They are tradable by all investors, providing a liquid and dividend-paying vehicle to invest in real estate. New and experienced investors can find a worthwhile addition to a balanced investment portfolio in REITs, which offer the combination of income and growth with real estate holdings.

Index Funds

Index funds are an exclusive and beneficial investment method, particularly for the new investor who is only dipping their toes into the enormous channels of the stock market. The idea of this money is to track the performance of a selected index, say the S&P 500, by investing in all or a representative sample of the securities in that index. This strategy provides an easy and effective method of attaining diversification, which is an important aspect in reducing risk within a portfolio.

Index funds have been developed based on the premise that it is easier said than done to get the better of the market. Most regular investors and investment funds have a desire to outperform the market averages by buying and selling successfully. Still, there is a great amount of research indicating that persistently outperforming might be uncommon. Index funds, in contrast, do not seek to beat the market but to track its performance, thus, in the long run, having better yields since there are fewer costs and expenses.

Index funds are one of the most relaxing advantages of index funds. The disadvantages of these funds are associated with costs, such as the fact that no research team is needed and there is no frequent trading, both of which save a lot of management fees. Cost savings on fees may accumulate in the long term, contributing to an increase in the overall returns on investments, as viewed by the shareholders. Moreover, the ease of index funds places them at a favorable point with those who are new to the investment game. One need not follow the share market constantly or change their trading strategy periodically: one can just set it and forget it, and even the fund will increase with time, requiring minimum care.

Another attractive quality is the availability of index funds. The amounts of money required to invest in these funds are relatively low and therefore are a viable option for the new investors. Additionally, it is possible to buy a fractional stake of an index fund in a huge number of brokerages, which means that the investor can choose investments diversely in spite of the small amount of initial capital.

Index funds are also commended to be very transparent. Investors are able to know what they are getting because such funds follow an identifiable index. The holdings of an index fund will be publicly known so that an investor can know what they are putting their money into. This openness assists in appreciating the exposure and the risk with regard to the fund.

Although index funds seem to be well off, it should be known that these types of funds are not risk-free. The returns produced by an index fund are directly linked to the returns provided by the followed index. As such, the index fund will go down in value, and the other market will go down. Nonetheless, index funds are diversified, and therefore, broad diversification can be used to dampen the effect of market fluctuations, as it does in individual stocks.

Basically, index funds provide a low-cost and more realistic method of investing in stocks. They jibe with the investment philosophy, stressing the long-term growth and risk management. Beginners consider index funds to be a reliable starting point that they can build on further as they grow in confidence and knowledge of the financial markets. They represent a prudent aspect of investment strategy that can enable an investor to meet their financial goals with minimum complications and expenditures frequently accompanying active management. Investors can, however, relish the merits of having the market grow at their expense, with less stress and, unlike the case amidst active funds, with less struggle.

Alternative Investments

Alternative investments provide a unique direction in the world of investment opportunities waiting to be explored for those people who want to diversify their portfolios with traditional stocks and bonds. These investments are broadly based and do not involve direct links with the normal public markets. Investors who shift to alternative investments are likely to experience an increase in returns and a reduction in risks incurred in standard investments.

Real estate is one of the most pronounced forms of real estate investments. Investing in real estate can manifest itself in a number of ways, with the investment property being acquired as residential or commercial property, real estate investment trusts (REITs), or via real estate crowdfunding. The investments are attractive because they can provide income via rental yields and increase the chances of appreciation in the future. But they, too, demand a hefty start-up cost and are subject to risks which include fluctuations in the market and troubles in the management of the property.

The other common type of alternative investments is in commodities, which involve tangible assets such as gold, oil, and agricultural products. It is usually said that commodities are a hedge against inflation since their prices usually increase when the prices of goods and services go up. The commodities field can be invested in by purchasing the commodity directly, using a futures arrangement, or a bundle of exchange-traded funds (ETFs). Commodities have the potential to generate decent returns but are also highly volatile because of geopolitical factors, impacts on the supply chain, and fluctuating involvement in consumer demand.

Another aspect regarding alternative investments would be the hedge funds, which are largely confined to the accredited investors owing to their complex and/or higher risk natures. A variety of methods are deployed to attain a higher rate of returns through such aspects as leverage, short selling, and derivative trading of these funds. Despite the ability of hedge funds to deliver great returns, they are associated with costs and little transparency compared to traditional investment vehicles.

Another important consideration in alternative investment is the activity called private equity, i.e., the buying out of non-public corporations or the shares in these corporations. The investors in private equity aim to enhance the performance of such firms in the long run and later sell the firm out or sell off their shares in the company through an initial public offering (IPO). This kind of investment is long-term with very little liquidity, and it may bring huge returns if the companies expand effectively.

Venture capital is a narrow area of practice of private equity that deals with funding enterprises at their initial stages and involves high growth rates. Venture capitalists give investments that are exchanged for shares or equities with the interest of banking on the high growth of such start-ups. Though venture capital may result in great returns, it is risky per se, owing to the lack of certainty about the success of new ventures.

Tangible assets such as art, collectibles, and others also constitute alternative investments. These are also assets that can be expected to increase many times over, and they do provide aesthetic pleasure, but they need knowledge to assess and may be very illiquid.

The use of substitute investments in a portfolio may present the capacity for diversification plus the prospect of high returns. However, investors need to do their homework before investing in these non-traditional investments and understand their risk-taking capacity, their investment horizon, and their liquidity requirements. It is necessary to study the peculiarities of every alternative investment type and the potential risks to make decisions and reach the investment objectives.

Chapter 9: Maximizing Returns with Dividends

How Dividends Work

Daughters refer to a peculiarity and, thus, a very profitable element of investments in the stock market. To most investors, especially the novices, the concept of dividends is like revealing a secret to their investment portfolios. By essence, a dividend refers to a share in the earnings of a firm handed down to firm holders; normally, it is paid in cash or other stocks. This distribution is one of the means through which companies give back whatever they have in the form of profit to the people who have invested in them in order to give them a reason to hold on to their shares in the long term.

Below is the attraction of dividends, having provided one with a continuous flow of revenue, which can be especially lucrative to individuals interested in supplementing their income or growing rich with time. Contrary to the rise of stock prices, where an investor has to sell to make some profit, the dividends provide a platform to continue earning without giving out shares. This feature is what attracts dividends to draw the attention of retirees or investors who need a constant source of income without the intention of selling assets.

The dividend receiving process has a number of important dates that investors have to know. The most important of these is the ex-dividend date, the deadline by which one must act to receive the next dividend payment. In the event that an investor buys a stock after this date, he/she would not get the dividend that will be paid next. After that, a dividend is paid on the basis of the review of the company's records, known as the record date. Lastly, the payment date is the actual date when the dividends are actually distributed to the shareholders, either in the form of cash or other shares.

As an example, let us assume that it is a blue-chip dividend-paying company that pays its dividends once a quarter. The shareholder in this company would get a stream of income (dividends) four times a year as an investor. Those payments are predictable, which can be a relief in an otherwise turbulent marketplace and the source of some financial stability.

Besides, investors could reinvest in a Dividend Reinvestment Plan (DRIP), in which dividends received are invested automatically in purchasing more shares of the stock. The power of the compound can be used in this reinvestment, which can drastically speed up the development of the portfolio of investments. Through rivaling the dividend, the investors are able to buy more shares without paying any taxes to their brokers, and this is one of the economic ways of investing in an increase in the shares held by the investor.

The effect of dividend reinvestment can be tremendous. Take the case of the investor who gets a dividend of $1,000 annually and reinvests the amount. After 10 + years, this portfolio, with reinvesting, can be a lot larger than taking the dividends as money. It is a plan that not only increases the net share ownership but also the dividend revenue, which in turn depends on the quantity of shares that attract more dividends.

Finally, dividends play a very important role in the stock market investments, as an income source and a growth instrument. They yield a physical payback on investment and stimulate a long-held vision, something desired by most investors who want to accumulate wealth over time. Knowing the idea behind dividends, when they are paid out, and how important reinvestment is, is likely to give investors some power to make good decisions and to improve their overall investment strategy.

Dividend Reinvestment Plans

Dividend reinvestment plans (DRIPs) are an exclusive opportunity that any investor can enjoy to use the power of compounding, where in DRIP, one can automatically invest a cash dividend into shares of the same stock. It is especially attractive to persons who feel comfortable using a long-term investment strategy, since this way a person can accumulate a long-term position without taking active trading decisions.

In DRIP, investors will choose to have the dividends paid in cash, but instead the investors have the option of letting the company reinvest such funds in buying more of their stocks or a decimal of the shares of their stocks. This reinvestment is automatic, meaning that there is usually no charge to reinvest, and this is a cheap means of accumulating holdings in the long term. The beauty of such a plan is that it is simple and able to take advantage of the compounding interest; that is, the earned money is once again invested in earning its own, therefore increasing the portfolio at a faster rate.

The key benefit of DRIPs is that they make it easy to calculate the dollar-cost average. The strategy of this type of investment is that a specific amount of a certain investment in dollars is purchased at a pre-determined interval, regardless of the share price. This could lead to a decrease in the average cost per share in the long term and minimize the effects of market volatility. As an example, when the stock price is high, the dividend will be paid out in fewer shares, and when the price is low, the dividend will be paid out in more shares. Such a methodological approach may result in a higher average price per share in the long run, which may increase the investor's return.

Also, usually investors have an option in DRIP to buy shares at a discount to the current market prices (this varies company by company). Such a discount may be a favorable aspect to an investor who wants to make the most out of his returns. In addition, most DRIPs allow reinvestment of dividends received without a charge to the investor, based on brokerage fees, allowing the investor to maximize the dollar amount, doing what he or she wants to do (working in the market).

The other major advantage is that DRIPs inculcate discipline in the investors. Automation helps to reduce the chances of making decisions that are purely emotive and influenced by the immediate changes witnessed in the market. This automation helps the investment strategy remain long-term oriented, stimulating the attitude that is not directed at short-term results.

However, one should take into consideration the tax consequences of DRIPs. Investors who have received dividends reinvested are still liable to pay taxes on that withholding amount on their actual calendar year, rather than on the period of the year when they do not receive the cash withheld. This implies that investors are expected to raise enough funds to meet the tax imposition, which may come as a big expense when not planned. Nevertheless, the tax factors do not generally work out against the investors who believe that the tax costs are correlated to the benefits of compounding and dollar-cost averaging.

To conclude, the idea of dividend reinvestment plans is a convenient way to develop an investment portfolio over time. Automatic reinvestment of dividends allows an investor to take advantage of both compound growth and dollar-cost averaging while also keeping transaction costs to a minimum and adhering to a disciplined investment plan. To the investors who are ready to grapple with the tax considerations, DRIPs are effective in meeting financial aspirations.

High Dividend Yield Stocks

Within the stock market field of investment, high-dividend-yielding stocks bear special interest to a number of investors, especially those interested in a continual flow of income. Such stocks are highly instrumental as well-established groups normally use them to offer investor dividends that are well above the average yield in the market. The feature makes them desirable investments to investors who are keen on generating income rather than capital gains.

Sectors like utilities, telecom, and consumer staples tend to generate high dividend yield stocks. These are stable industries in that continuous cash flow is available and enables constant payment of dividends. Firms in these industries are likely to possess well-established business strategies with stable profits; thus, they are able to give a considerable share of their profit as dividends to stockholders. It is this stability that is most attractive to risk-averse investors who add a premium to the dependability of a consistent income.

Investors focusing on high dividend yield stocks ought to research the long-term viability of the dividend. The financial guidance to keep in mind is that the high yield might look like a red flag, indicating that the company was in financial trouble or was experiencing a sudden dividend growth. An analysis of the payout ratio of the firm is important to find out the balance between the dividend amount paid and the net income. A large payout ratio could indicate that the organization may be paying out more than it can comfortably pay without running a risk of its dividend being cut in the future.

The other observation is the company's track record in relation to dividend payments. The tendency to be able to sustain or grow upon their dividends over time is often a good sign of financial soundness and a commitment of management to the return of value, including the shareholders. These may often be companies termed as dividend aristocrats, which are those companies that have raised their dividend payouts every year over the last 25 years or more. Investors looking to achieve their dividend-oriented goals usually target companies.

Nonetheless, it is not risk-free investing in high-dividend-yield stocks. Interest rate movements can be a sensitive subject for these stocks. An increase in the interest rates makes a fixed income that one gets as a dividend less appealing than the new bonds yielding as the interest rates do, which is likely to cause falling stock prices. There is also the fact that dividend-paying companies that record huge dividend yields may not be able to grow to the same extent since they may not be able to plow a lot of their profit into their business ventures, opting to distribute profits among shareholders.

The investors will also need to know the tax implications of dividend income. The dividends may, in certain cases, be taxed at even a higher rate than capital gains based on the taxation bracket of the investor and the taxation policies of a country, and this may end up impacting the net amount of income earned out of these investments.

Risks need to be minimized by diversifying into different sectors and geographical locations. The strategy can be useful to hedge against cyclical declines in the sector and give a more consistent total payoff. Moreover, the inclusion of high dividend yield stock in a portfolio with growth stock may be a good combination, as it will provide the portfolio with a potential income and capital gains to satisfy short-term income requirements and long-term growth.

In conclusion, high dividend yield stocks, although a decent part of a diversified investment portfolio, have to be carefully evaluated and paid due attention to. The evaluation of dividend sustainability, the consideration of economic effects of influences, and the convenient tax implications will help an investor make reasonable choices that will be consistent with their financial objectives.

Building a Dividend Portfolio

Building a dividend-focused portfolio is a tactical exercise that seeks to build a stream of income, but at the same time, enjoy possible capital gains over time. This form of investment is not only profitable in the sense that it provides a steady income, but also in the sense that compounding works wonders when the dividend is reinvested.

First of all, it is essential to realize the very idea of dividend investing. Dividends refer to shares of a company's earnings that are paid to shareholders (quarterly in most cases). Paying companies are usually mature, and their cash flow is stable and profitable, which is why they are popular with investors in need of stable income flows. Such firms are commonly known as Dividend Aristocrats, a term used to describe firms that have been able to record an increase in their dividend payments to shareholders over a number of decades.

To reduce its risk, a good dividend portfolio must represent different sectors. These involve the choice of picking stocks in sectors like utility, consumer staples, and telecommunications industries, which have, over time, been identified as having been consistent with high dividends. The point is to find the balance between the dividend growth capability and high dividend yields. High-yielding stocks can yield instant income, whereas dividend-growing stocks can deliver constantly enhancing income, which may beat inflation.

In working out a portfolio of dividend stocks, it is essential to evaluate the financial foundations of the prospective holdings. Important ones are the dividend yield, payout ratio, and the history of dividend payments and dividend increases. An acceptable sustainable payout ratio, which denotes the rate of profit that is being paid as dividends, is equal to 50 percent or less. This implies that the firm will not be distributing a lot of its income in terms of dividends, leaving it with sufficient amounts with which it can again reinvest in growth opportunities, hence resulting in future dividends being raised.

The second thing is, do you want to invest in individual stocks or exchange-traded funds (ETFs) that take the dividend as their theme? Although individual stocks have the potential for greater returns and the ability to control particular investments, dividend ETFs have the benefits of immediate diversification and reduced risk by holding a selection of dividend-paying stocks. One of the main benefits of ETFs is that they are especially useful to novice investors or those who have little time to invest.

Another consideration is reinvestment of dividends in terms of the Dividend Reinvestment Plan (DRIP). DRIPs enable one to have dividends automatically allocated to buy more stocks in the company, returning on profit. This strategy can go a long way to improving the performance of a dividend portfolio, and this is even more so when the strategy is employed as a long-term measure.

One must be conscious of the tax provisions related to the dividends. Qualified dividends are ordinary income that are taxed at a lower rate than regular income, when they satisfy the IRS requirements as qualified dividends. Such knowledge on how to treat the taxes can aid in maximizing the net returns of a dividend portfolio.

Lastly, the portfolio should be reviewed and rebalanced periodically in order to be consistent with the investment objectives and risk tolerance. This will involve tracking the stock performance, allocating sectors and sitting them accordingly, in order to take advantage of the fluctuating market system, or changes in company performance. With effective management and emphasis on quality, a dividend portfolio has the potential to generate stable and increasing dividend income that may support the current financial requirements of the investor. It can help them accumulate wealth over a long period.

Creating a Vision for Your Career

For career development, deciding on your desired future is very important for accomplishing your career goals. Having this vision helps clear a direction when facing difficulties in career advancement. You need to start by setting challenging yet attainable goals for your journey. They act as markers, guiding the creation of a work path that fits your dreams and exists in the marketplace.

To see your way forward in a career, you need to reflect on yourself and think ahead. This means thinking ahead about what you want in your career and where you hope to end up. Knowledge of what talents, interests, and values are most important to an individual builds the solid foundation for a great career vision. Those who choose clear goals find it easier to follow the right path, as well as to keep motivated and dedicated.

Having a clear reason for your future in your career drives motivation. It serves to guide individuals in what direction to move and what objectives matter most. Being clear supports making good choices so that every action contributes to the overall aim. In addition, a solid vision makes one more flexible since it inspires people during hard times, enabling them to cope with problems more strongly.

To achieve your hopes, you must make sure your daily activities follow your vision. Sometimes, you review your progress and change your strategies depending on what is happening now. Using a flexible method, individuals ensure their everyday activities support their big-picture career plans. Having everything aligned means team members feel more committed and prouder of their progress as they reach their targets.

More examples of people having successful careers by planning their careers suggest the strength of having a clear vision early. Notice how a business owner's commitment to a mission leads to a flourishing startup or how a creative worker succeeds with clear and well-defined career steps. From what we see, making sure you have an established vision is essential since it offers direction to people working towards their dreams.

In brief, to design a career vision, you need to link who you are now with where you want to head in the future. It's all about creating a plan that you enjoy doing and that's reachable so your career meets both your career goals and what matters to you. When individuals act in line with what they have planned and what they want from their careers, they can turn their dreams into real success.

Chapter 10: Leveraging Technology in Investing

Utilizing Online Platforms

Online investment has become a necessity in the contemporary environment of investments that are conducted through the stock market, and this has become a key aspect in tools that new and existing investors use. The digital era has led to a change in the way we read, interpret, and make trades, and a beginner must get to tip-toe on the features and benefits of these interfaces to allow him/to have a better experience.

Investing online is a way to enter the stock market world, whereby one is able to now access the stock market fully at a new level of convenience and capability. These platforms seem like a bridge that allows individual investors to immerse themselves in a previously closed world of financial possibilities, dominated by professional brokers and institutional investors. They also provide an easy-to-use platform where it is possible to research stocks, make trades, and track portfolios on a real-time basis.

The liberalization of financial information can be said to be one of the most important advantages of using online platforms. These websites concentrate on such an abundance of information, from current stock rates to full-fledged financial statements, which have never been readily available to anyone. Such openness gives investors the information they need to make wise investing decisions, independent of third-party advice, and makes this environment of investing more self-reliant.

In addition, online resources tend to blend with educational materials of low complexity. These materials include tutorials and webinars, in-depth articles, as well as practical forums, which an amateur investor can familiarize themselves with what it means to become a stock investor, as well as Proprietary Stratagems. In this type of learning environment, people have the freedom to develop skills and confidence at their own pace with the support of like-minded people.

The other key attributes of online platforms are speed and efficiency in making trades. High brokerage fees, together with minimum investments, which were considered traditional barriers to entry, are heavily reduced or completely removed. Several trading websites allow commission-free trading, which allows buying shares even with small investments. This openness will give rise to more individuals to take part in the stock market, embracing an open culture of inclusivity and fiscal literacy.

Another important element that online platforms introduce is automation. Investors have the option of establishing automated investments, in which money is consistently invested in a chosen number of stocks or exchange-traded funds (ETFs). Such a set-it-and-forget-it idea assists the investor to maintain a disciplined investing strategy, as opposed to making an emotional or impulsive decision on how they should trade. Automation eliminates the guesswork of investing every time, and, instead, reaps the benefit of the diamond of dollar-cost averaging and compounded time over the long term.

Moreover, a great number of Web-based services also provide portfolio analysis and performance monitoring. Investors are able to track their investment easily, trigger alerts when a particular market condition is met, and determine when adjustments should be made to their portfolio. These tools give priceless indications on where the markets are doing great and where they require modifications, and the investors are able to streamline their strategies to suit their financial targets.

As a conclusion, investing in the stock market online has changed the game since it offers tools, resources, and peers to empower people to take control of their financial future. With the further development of the financial environment, these platforms will gain more and more importance in the development of the investment policy of future generations and, therefore, they will remain a critical part of the toolkit of any novice investor.

Investment Apps and Tools

The world of investing in the stock markets has changed over the centuries, where technology has transformed the manner in which investors in stock markets access and maintain their investment portfolios in the contemporary world. With the introduction of investment applications and tools, we have come into an era of democratized investing where both beginners and experienced investors have added access to investments. These online applications provide so many features that make the investment process easy and the decision-making process more straightforward. They allow people to monitor what they invest in without any hassles.

The reason is that investment apps are the must-have tools when one has decided to begin their investing career, but with ease and simplicity that was never part of the stock market. The apps have user-friendly interfaces, which enable investors to purchase and sell stocks, ETFs, and other securities by simply tapping their smartphone devices. They provide up-to-date information, news, and pertinent market commentaries, thus enabling investors to make sound decisions based on current events.

Among the greatest opportunities of investment apps is that it is possible to begin investing with little money. A large number of platforms have a fractional stock purchase option, which implies that investors can purchase a small piece of a stock as opposed to a single share. This feature has given people who might not be in a position to spend large sums of money the opportunity to grow into diversified portfolios slowly.

Besides the trading features, investment apps have education resources that provide novices with the rudiments of investing. These materials may include papers and video lessons, as well as online courses that would address financial planning, asset allocation, and risk management. Through these tools, these apps act as a learning platform where people can develop confidence and a store of knowledge when using the stock market.

Another progressive tool that has become popular among the hands-off-seeker investors is robo-advisors. Such online platforms employ computer algorithms to develop and handle investment algorithms in accordance with a person's risk tolerance, financial goals, and time horizon. Robo-advisors also provide automated rebalancing and tax-loss harvesting that keep the portfolios in line with the goal of the user and at the same time reduce the tax burden. Due to the low cost and convenience, robo-advisors have become an appealing choice among users, who like to set and forget.

In addition, investment applications and tools include the powerful functionality of tracking performance, which enables investors to track their portfolio's growth over time. The user may see in detail how his investments are doing, with such indicators as total return, annualized return, and dividend yield. These insights will allow investment generators to evaluate their advances towards their financial objectives and alter the required strategies.

In a bid to improve security, most investment apps are designed with these advanced security features, such as two-factor authentication and encryption. All these attributes make the personal and financial data of the users secure, therefore ensuring the reliability of the digital investing resources.

To sum up, investment apps and tools have changed how people buy or sell stock. These platforms have assumed a more accessible and manageable place in everyone's lives by incorporating aspects of ease of use, educational programs, and advanced capabilities such as robo-advisors and performance monitoring. Investing today, whether as an occasional first-time buyer using fractional shares or as a more experienced user of automated portfolio management, as it is now, if you do not use digital tools, then chances are you are at a significant disadvantage compared to those who do.

Automated Investing

Automation in the investment field has gotten impressive momentum, and few people would be surprised by what automation offers and delivers. Automated investing is a new and efficient method that uses technology to facilitate investment, making it easy to comprehend by even investors who are new to the field, as well as busy people involved. Through the applications of automated systems, an investor can develop a disciplined approach that reduces human error and concurrently offers maximum payoff.

The essence of automated investing rests on the use of the phrase, set it and forget it. This plan promotes the idea of setting a prepared strategy and letting the automated program perform this strategy regularly, and therefore minimizing the effects of emotional decisions made in response to market trends. One of the hazards of investing can also be called emotional investment and can be identified as the tendency to buy on an impulse when markets are up and to sell aggressively when times are bad. Automation can easily avoid such falls by sticking to a rule that is based on a systematic approach, so that any short-term volatility of the stock prices in the marketplace cannot sway it.

The incorporation of robo-advisors can be listed among the most notable instruments of automated investing. Such digital platforms provide algorithm-based financial planning solutions that have little manual involvement. Robo-advisors consider an investor's financial target, risk tolerance, and time horizon in order to develop a diversified portfolio, which contributes to their objectives. They constantly track and adjust the portfolio so as to maintain the desired asset allocation, and this will ensure that the investment strategy is still on track. The hands-off style is also attractive to individuals with either no time to spend managing or possessing any experience in the management of investments.

Besides, automated investing is not restricted to robo-advisors. Many brokerages provide facilities for automatic payment and reinvestment. Automatic contributions allow the investor to make a specific amount of recording on a routine basis to the investment account, which can stimulate the discipline of investment savings and dollar-cost averaging. This is investing a certain amount set periodically, no matter what the market is like at the moment, which can limit the effect of the market in the long run.

Another area of automation is dividend reinvestment plans (DRIPS), which allow the investor to automatically reinvest the money obtained by the dividends into other stocks or funds of the same stock. This reinvestment may increase the reinvestment effect even more, and over time, the investment may grow very large. Automating the reinvestment of the dividends will mean that the investors will be confident that their dividends will be reinvested within a due time and without manual interference.

Automated investing has a number of advantages. It provides a structured method that minimizes the chances of making impulsive judgments in response to the mood of the market. It also saves time and energy as people can be occupied with other parts of their lives, but their investment will be handled on a regular basis. Automation brings some comfort to the novice investor who can be sure that he operates his assets in accordance with a stable, objective plan.

Automated investing has drawbacks, as well as benefits. It might not provide the personal approach and flexibility that some investors want, particularly those who like to be more hands-on. Also, as much as automation would be effective in handling routine duties, it might never be prepared to cope with complex financial situations or unpredictable market changes that necessitate inputs of human judgment.

To sum up, automated investing is a tremendous step towards the sphere of personal Finance that offers a convenient solution to the problem of investing with minimum time wasted. Using the power of technology, an investor can develop a solid investment plan that will support his or her objectives, minimize the influence of emotion, and enable long-term financial development. The opportunities and the features of automated investing will continue to increase, and as the technology progresses, one will find the journey to financial independence even easier.

Staying Informed with Technology

Stock market investing is one of the fields in which it is crucial to be updated, and technology, in its turn, becomes an irreplaceable partner in it. The modern world is characterized by the fact that investors can get access to a plethora of information and resources on the digital market at an exceptionally fast pace. The online world has changed the way investors collect, measure, and take action regarding market information. Those who want to venture into the market must fully utilize the opportunities presented by the digital era.

Probably the greatest technological advantage of investing is the live market information. With the help of mobile applications and online tools, investors all over the world can monitor the price of a stock, market trends, and current events in the commercial world. Such immediacy enables the investors to make a better decision with the updated information, thus facing little or no chance of using outdated or second-hand information. Money apps such as Yahoo Finance, Google Finance, and those used by specific brokers give access to detailed data, news, and analysis instruments that play a substantial role in making valid investment decisions.

In addition, technology has made more complicated analysis tools belonging to the domain of professional traders more democratic. Platforms have since come with technical analysis charts, financial indicators, and predictive algorithms that give investors a more precise answer on how to judge a prospective investment. All these tools allow even inexperienced investors to engage in detailed research and evaluation, and make them more able to make decisions analytically.

Moreover, the emergence of social media and online communities has opened up new opportunities for investors to share ideas and educate each other. Reddit and Twitter are good examples of communities where investors share market trends, post stock recommendations, and seek peer support. They can be very useful in accessing and listening to the different points of view. Still, it matters a lot that the investor carefully considers the sources and does not fall into the trap of the hype and misinformation.

The incorporation of technology into investing also embraces the process of automating trade processes. To make the process of investment management automatic, robo-advisors have become a well-established mode of automation to allow services to include portfolio rebalancing, tax-loss harvesting, and so on, without active human control. This auto-investing not only saves time but also contributes to having a disciplined approach to investment as it eliminates the emotional aspect of decision-making.

More so, technology helps to undertake ongoing learning and skills improvement. There are online courses, webinars, and podcasts that offer an easy way to learn more about every detail of investing, from the simplest idea of investing to complex techniques. Investors will only have the option of customizing their learning to suit their time and desire, and the fast-growing market will always cover them.

In order to utilize technology, investors are supposed to have a proactive approach. It includes alerting major market indicators, frequent updates of watchlists, and the use of digital technology to monitor investment performance. By staying informed and active, investors are able to cope more easily with complicated market conditions and become better financially literate.

To sum it up, technology can be an invaluable tool in the venture of an investor, being used wisely as possible, it can greatly augment their capability of remaining informed and being able to make a strategic decision. It is through adopting such digital forces that investors may be able to have a competitive advantage, making them properly eligible to realize their monetary targets in the evolving global share market investing.

CHAPTER 11: TAX IMPLICATIONS OF INVESTING

Understanding Capital Gains Tax

The capital gains tax is also the core knowledge one needs to have down the line to be a beginner in stock market investing. This levy is imposed when the revenues of a sold asset have been obtained, and thus it is a key concept generating investment decisions and economic performance. There are mainly two, namely, short-term capital gain tax and long-term capital gain tax, based on the duration of the holding of the asset. Short-term capital gains are capital gains earned on assets that have been held for a year or less and are taxed at the ordinary income tax rates, which are much higher than the taxes on long-term capital gains. On the other hand, the long-term capital gains (invested for more than 1 year) also have lower tax, which encourages investors to keep their investments longer.

The very important difference between realized and unrealized gains is in the determination of whether taxation is payable. An increase in the value of an asset not sold does not count as a gain; hence, it is not taxable. Paper profits:

Unrealized gains are not subject to taxation until the sale of an asset, and investors can defer their payment of taxes and still may enjoy additional appreciation of the assets. This distinction highlights the significance of planning in the timing of asset sales to obtain optimistic after-tax returns.

There are many wrong ideas as far as capital gains tax is concerned, and most especially by non-initiates. Also, the assumption that taxes on paper profits can occur is considered one of the myths, and it may cause anxiety and prevent reasonable investments. There is also the sore misconception that keeping investments indefinitely without incurring any tax is possible, not considering that in the due course of life, investments will have to be converted into cash either on retirement or towards any other financial need.

In order to keep the administrative costs of capital gains taxes to a minimum, an investor must be keen to record all their transactions well, i.e., by keeping records on purchase prices, the price of sale, and the periods of holding. This is very essential when it comes to tax reporting, as it can make it easier during the tax season. These transactions are described in such a form as 1099-B, which is used by brokers and helps to determine the value of the capital gains tax to be paid.

There are legal and practical ways to reduce capital gains taxes. Tax-loss harvesting is one such strategy whereby investors are able to sell securities at a loss to gather up the gains they had acquired on other investments, where the income earned is liable to be taxed. The other thing they can do is invest in preferred tax accounts such as IRAs and 401 (k) s, where money invested grows without taxation or tax-deferred until the time of draw.

In conclusion, it can be said that proper knowledge and handling of capital gains tax can greatly improve the investor's investment strategy, allowing the investor to make the correct decision and gain as much net income as possible throughout the entire process. Investors can use several strategies to make the best use of capital gains tax, such as by taking into account the timing of asset sales, tactics implemented by using a tax-advantaged account, and tax-loss harvesting. In this way, such individuals can elaborate on how to make wise use of making money on the market without falling foul of capital gains tax. This information can enable the investor to build strategies that fit investment aspirations so that the investment experience entails a more secure and prosperous future.

It is crucial to understand the intricacies of capital gains tax, as any investor would want to maximize his or her portfolio. Making tax planning part of their investment strategy, beginners not only minimize tax expenses but also improve their general financial planning, which will predetermine their future success in the stock market.

Tax-Advantaged Accounts

To get started exploring the world of tax-advantaged accounts could be a crucial move towards earning the maximum profits on your investments at the lowest taxes. Such accounts, e.g., Individual Retirement Accounts (IRAs) and 401(k)s, are designed to give you some tax advantages which, in the long term, can add greatly to your savings. The ideas of the subtleties of these accounts will assist you in making wise choices depending on the plans of your retirement and financial status.

The main benefit of the accounts is their taxation treatment. The traditional IRA and 401(k) give you an opportunity to place pre-tax money in them, and this decreases your annual taxable earnings. This is to enable you to pay tax on the contribution at a rate that is later in your retirement years, when there is a chance that you may fall into a cheaper tax bracket. Roth IRAs can also be used; on the other hand, they have a different advantage in that they are funded with after-tax dollars, making withdrawals in retirement are tax-free. This may be quite beneficial when you believe that you will be in a higher tax bracket in the future.

The choice of the account would depend on a number of factors such as your level of income, whether you are employed or not, and your retirement plan. An example is that of a Traditional IRA, which can be appropriate in case you need tax relief now and project that your income will decline in your retirement. On the other hand, a Roth IRA account would prove better when you favor tax-free growth and anticipate greater income in the future. It is important to know how much one owes, how much one can contribute, and on what basis one is eligible to contribute. To take an example, Roth IRA has limits on incomes that may not allow higher earners to make direct contributions; this is compared to 401(k)s that are usually provided by employers, and they mostly come with the advantage of a company contribution.

It may be accessible to open and keep a tax-favored account, though it can be quite simple to see. Most brokerage houses and financial institutions make it simple to have an IRA through online procedures. When choosing a 401(k), your employer usually runs the necessary arrangements with the provider of their choice. Interestingly, one should think about automating the contributions so that the money could be invested regularly and allow the power of compound interest to work. A modest, steady amount can become considerable with time, even because of the phenomenon of compounding.

Failing to maximize the employer match to the 401(k) is one of the most frequent mistakes that investors make. This is basically free and can make you save a lot of money in your retirement. One should not make the mistake of taking early withdrawals as they attract penalties and cancel the tax bonus attached to such accounts. It is important to learn the rules pertaining to withdrawals, including the necessary minimum distribution (RMD) of Traditional IRA and the 401(k), since this will limit the unnecessary tallying of fines.

To get the best out of the tax-advantaged accounts, one is supposed to review one's portfolio and account selection periodically, depending on the improvement of one's financial condition and objectives. This will make sure that you are doing what you need to do to make your goals, as far as retirement is concerned, and the tax benefits you are entitled to take as much advantage of as possible. As an investor who is still exploring the world of investing or a long-practicing investor, adding tax-advantaged accounts to your financial plan may be a smart choice in the long run.

Tax-Loss Harvesting

The rules of investing in the stock market are not only rules of making the maximum levels of profit, but also the rules of how to minimize losses. Tax-loss harvesting is one of those strategies that an investor, especially a novice, can utilize. The method is an effective way of helping to minimize taxable income through selling securities at a loss in order to settle capital gains on alternative investments.

Tax-loss harvesting is an approach that exploits the volatility of the stock market. Investors may also intentionally sell investments that have fallen in value to enable them to realize losses that may then be offset by gains in other parts of their portfolio. Such a process will not only eliminate the overall amount of tax that is due but also enable the investor to keep their investment strategy by purchasing another asset of a similar nature, and hence keep the portfolio in tandem with their long-term direction.

The merits of tax-loss harvesting can be almost summed up: provided that the investor is able to sell a certain security at a lower price than he /she purchased it initially, he/she would get the opportunity to deduct the capital gains tax of the profitable investment and thus pay less tax. This is especially advantageous for investors since they can reduce their tax brackets and determine whether or not the losses and gains are realized.

Nevertheless, there are complexities with regard to the strategy. The investors should pay attention to the wash-sale rule, which states that it is not possible to buy the same security or another one having practically the same content within 30 days before or after the sale. The idea behind this rule is that it will not allow investors to edge in a claim of tax deduction without making a substantial change in their stock. The approach to circumvent it is for investors to be interested in buying similar, but not the same, securities that would enable their portfolio to be balanced and with expected degrees of risk.

Tax-loss harvesting needs the close observation of market trends and asset timing strategies. It is best to operate in a volatile market where fluctuations in prices offer a great opportunity to make losses accessible. The investors are able to enjoy the optimum advantage of tax-loss harvesting by paying attention to their portfolio and, accordingly, being able to respond immediately when the market goes down in order to benefit.

In addition to the short-term tax advantages, tax-loss harvesting may lead to an improvement in the overall financial strategy of an investor. Through systematic rebalancing and changing of the portfolio, investors can guarantee that their portfolio is diversified and in line with their financial aims. This periodic evaluation assists in the determination of poorly performing holdings and gives one a chance to rebalance investments, thus streamlining the performance of the portfolio.

Tax-loss harvesting may appear to be a complex notion to a beginner, though it is an organized way to address the taxation of investments. New investors should consider getting acquainted with their current taxation situation and discussing it with a tax expert to make the strategy custom to their needs. This way, they will be able to incorporate the idea of tax-loss harvesting into their comprehensive investment strategy and transform potential losses into opportunities as well.

To conclude, tax-loss harvesting can be an effective instrument for those investors who would like to reduce the effects of capital gains taxes. Through an intentional recognition of losses and subsequent reinvesting them in the related asset types, investors may keep their portfolio potential intact with a decrease in taxable income. The method will not only be helpful in saving on taxation, but it will also keep the portfolio management in a more disciplined domain, leading toward a stronger and resilient investment strategy.

Planning for Tax Efficiency

Stock market investing is a process that entails acquiring and disposing of shares not only to make purchases and achieve profits, but also to plan the taxation made on such activities properly. Knowledge of the intricacies involved in tax efficiency is vital in terms of ascertaining maximum returns and liability reduction. The issue at the center of tax efficiency is that of capital gains, which represents the profits gained upon selling investments like stocks. The two types of capital gains are short-term and long-term, which have different tax rates. The short-term gains are taxed as ordinary income, which is usually much higher than the long-term capital gains rate charged on assets sold after the year.

Another underlying aspect is the difference between realized and unrealized gains. Realized gains are taxed upon realizing the gains or when an asset realizes a gain through its sale. On the other hand, gains that had not been realized, sometimes termed as paper profits, are not subjected to taxation until the asset being realized is sold. The knowledge can enable the investors to make the right choices on the time they are going to sell their assets, which would result in a postponement of taxes through long-term holding of the investments.

Another area that needs tax planning is dividend income. Dividends may be either ordinary or qualified, and qualified dividends are usually at the preferential long-term capital gains rate. Knowledge of these classifications can assist investors in maximizing the taxation treatment of dividend income.

Investors ought to keep good records in order to plan well on tax efficiency. These involve monitoring the cost bases of purchases, sales, and holding of each investment, and maintaining all the tax forms, including 1099-DIV and 1099-B, among others, as they provide the investors with the ability to get ready in the tax season and having the ability to report income and gains of the investments.

Tax-favored accounts, including IRAs and 401 (k), provide great benefits in terms of tax efficiency. Traditional IRAs and 401(k)s have pre-tax contribution, which decreases one-year contribution taxable income, and Roth IRAs have tax-free growth and distributions during retirement. It is also important to know the contribution limits, the tax implications, and withdrawal provisions of each kind of account so as to maximize the benefits of such accounts.

Tactical ways to reduce taxes would be to keep investments for more than a year to avail the advantages of lower rates of long-term capital gains, tax-loss harvesting where gains are offset using losses, and selection of tax-efficient investment vehicles like index funds and ETFs. Tax-loss harvesting refers to the practice of selling investments at a loss to cover the gains made in other areas, thus lessening the total taxable income.

Those strategies can also boost the tax efficiency of an investment when they are included as part of an organized operation. The tax implication must be taken into consideration anytime one is debating whether to hold or sell. Through the systematic implementation of these concepts, investors will have a minimized tax and a better total portfolio performance.

Finally, tax efficiency planning has to be proactive. It is crucial to audit the investment portfolios routinely, remain knowledgeable about the shifts in taxation laws, and discuss the tax laws with tax professionals. Prudent planning and concerted action enable the investors to deal with the intricacies of taxation in such a way that the benefits of their investment are fully realized and the tax burden is also reduced to a minimum.

CHAPTER 12: AVOIDING COMMON INVESTMENT PITFALLS

Recognizing Scams and Frauds

There are numerous scams and frauds in the stock market trading world, where the urge to become a successful investor at a short time may allow people to make decisions without researching before and when they think they can make a lot of money in a short period, without actually taking time to calculate what they want to do. It is important to be aware of such pitfalls when you are an investor who wants to save their or her earned money and apply wise decisions.

Frauds in the stock market are usually disguised as a good opportunity, thus becoming hard to detect at a glance. Among the most widely applied schemes by the fraudsters is the offer of a sure profit. This alone is a significant red flag because no honest investment can promise returns since the market is prone to risk. Also, any payment request by unusual means that includes cryptocurrency deals, gift cards, etc., must be treated as a red flag since most of the time, a provider uses such methods to ensure funds are not traceable and are gone for good.

Another defining feature of a fraudulent scheme is a high-pressure sales tactic. The use of words such as act now or you miss out is meant to help build urgency, which puts pressure on people to make hurried decisions without considering them carefully. The need to act immediately goes around the logical reasoning required to evaluate the validity of an investment offering.

The digital era has added new grounds for fraud, especially on social sites and Internet communities. Pandemic stock tips and celebrity endorsements can lead to a buying spree, but the affected investing decisions are typically less informed than one might expect. This is the phenomenon of FOMO (fear of missing out) when people can spontaneously make purchases at excessive prices, subsequently losing money when the hype dies out.

Investors must devise a mechanism for verifying the legitimacy of any investment opportunity in order to protect themselves against such threats. An actionable list of a scam filter may prove to be of great help. Some of the steps in this checklist can include doing research about the reputation of the company or the advisor and checking on whether there are any regulatory or other actions or complaints against them, and also referring to official lists of investor alerts by the relevant regulatory agencies, such as the SEC or FINRA.

The cautionary tales happening to people in the real world tragically remind us of the chance to lose something.

Experienced investors are not an exception to the well-orchestrated schemes. The most popular is the so-called pump-and-dump scheme in which scammers artificially raise the price of a stock and then sell their shares, leaving gullible investors with stock that has no value.

One should be aware of the scams and prevent them through education and alertness. Investors can self-protect by knowing the most common tricks by theft artists and also remaining skeptical. Keeping knowledge of the current scams and fraud tricks up to date is also very important, as these tricks change with time.

To sum up, being able to identify scams and frauds is valuable to every investor. With timely information, caution, and a well-organized strategy in verifying investment opportunities, one is likely to make sure that he/she is in control of the stock market at higher levels of safety. Such vigilance not only preserves financial resources but also adds to a more secure and reliable market background.

Avoiding Emotional Traps

The stock market is a complicated place to be, more so if one is a novice and is likely to fall into a morass of emotional traps. Panic selling or having been caught up in the fear of missing out (FOMO) are only a few traps that can defeat the best-laid investment plans. It is important to know such emotional traps, as well as how to avoid them, to be a consistent and rational investor.

FOMO is one of the most widely spread emotional traps. This is because when investors jump onto the bandwagon of a popular stock, they tend to do so when the stock is at its highest mark due to the fear of missing out on the profits that may come with it. The activity is often supported by social media and shocking stories where quick profits are highlighted, making the situation urgent and exciting. However, with such inflated prices, such purchases would likely be a loss as far as the correction in the market goes.

Another major trap is panic selling; this is mostly induced by the fall of the markets. With the stock prices starting to fall, fear and anxiety may lead investors to sell whatever they have to save their losses. This counterattack strategy leads to making losses most of the time, but it would have been easy to avoid it by responding in a less extremist way. The investors are advised not to panic by selling their investments, but instead hold the initial plans of their investments and reflect on their long-term objectives. This assists in coming to terms with oneself and not being hasty in making decisions.

Emotional investing also has much to do with herd mentality. This is whereby people would copy the behavior of a bigger group of people and think that the herd must have been acting out of great knowledge. Nevertheless, this causes investing in over-appreciated shares or selling at stock market lows, both of which tend to harm the portfolio of an investor.

Another trap that can ensnare investors is revenge trading. Having suffered a loss, other investors may feel the urge to recoup the lost funds, and therefore, they end up trading at higher risks. This will create a loop of losses since one will make decisions based on emotions instead of a proper strategy.

To avoid all these emotional pitfalls, there is a need to introduce countermeasures that will encourage rational decisions. Among the ways is the so-called emotional circuit breakers, which is an awesome tactical approach to taking time and contemplating prior to making incautious choices. To give an example, the so-called 5-minute rule proposes leaving the screen during the trade and taking 5 minutes before performing the transaction. This short break may give the insight required to make better decisions.

Also, prepared answers may be useful. The advice to remind oneself of long-term goals is to create statements that reiterate core investment strategy, such as checking my initial course of action before doing anything, which assists investors in warding off the temptation to make decisions based on emotions.

The other common trick of not getting into the emotional trap is developing a support system. This may include becoming an accountability partner with a fellow investor who may be able to offer you an opinion and encourage you to be disciplined in the turbulent state of a volatile market. Meeting with an accountability partner can be one way to build smart investing behaviors and receive a feeling of togetherness.

Ultimately, the combination of awareness, preparation, and discipline is also required to avoid emotional traps. As long as investors are aware of the psychological phenomena taking place and can counteract those, they will remain on a level path and ultimately concentrate on reaching their financial objectives.

Overcoming Analysis Paralysis

The phenomenon of analysis paralysis is a typical impediment found in stock market investing, and it is a trap that many novice investors usually get caught up in. The condition of overthinking can slow down the decision-making process, resulting in lost opportunities and more anxiety. The solution to this barrier is to make the process of conducting research easy and to create a feeling of assurance, even when making decisions with reduced information.

Even a novice is often overwhelmed by the immense amount of information and its interpretation. The internet is flooded with charts, measures, thoughts, and everything that suggests they have the answer to successful investing. This avalanche of information may make it hard to identify and decide on what is indeed necessary, causing a chain of continuous research without practical conclusions. In order to get out of this loop, it is also vital to build an efficient stock assessment routine.

An efficient approach is the implementation of a brief and time-saving checklist, which is used to perform fast evaluations. The style underlines the necessity of paying attention primarily to such things as the financial well-being of a company, its market performance, and current news. Through the reduction in the criteria, the investors would make the right decisions without being stuck with irrelevant information. The teaching method not only helps save time but also lightens the mental burden, which helps the learner to perform their actions clearly and with confidence.

An obvious example wherein this method can be applied is by taking a familiar stock, say Apple, and doing a simplified checklist. One can have a review of industry position, an overview of the company, recent updates, and some of the basic valuation measurements in a few minutes. The quick scouting enables the investor to make up his mind faster without experiencing the paralysis of analysis, where everything is examined to death.

Furthermore, templates and forms that can be downloaded may be a good way of practical practice. This material offers a systematic way of carrying out research and thus promotes consistency and the formation of evaluation habits. Consistent use of such tools would also enable beginners to form a habit that would enable them to demystify stock research and gain confidence in the long run.

To use real-life examples and situations is also helpful. As an example, it is possible to compare the experience of skimming a stock in such a period as five minutes with hours of uncertainty and emphasize the benefits of a simplified scheme. It is because of this comparison that the idea of beginning with a basic idea is better than not beginning at all.

Finally, it is important to get out of analysis paralysis by changing the mentality. It is all about shoving off the thought that one has to get it right to achieve success in the field of investing. It is a better option to make steps towards action, even though you have limited knowledge, than to leave it to cross your fingers, waiting for the mythical perfect decision. However, using an efficient research flow and handy tools, a novice user can get around the difficulties of the stock market with more ease and comfort. Not only is this initiative helpful in assuaging the dangers of indecisiveness, but it also creates a more constructive, as well as more lucrative, way to invest.

Sticking to Your Plan

In the context of stock market investments, one thing that cannot be avoided is patient determination to stick to what you have invested. Investing at times can be a roller coaster ride with stalls and a ride powered by extreme market trends and the overabundance of information with a press of a button. Many would like to think that successful investors are those who have managed to maintain their convictions as they continued doing what they did, rather than giving in to the temptation of market gyrations.

Your initial move toward sticking with your investment plan is to clearly define your goals and the timeframe within which they should be accomplished. It is your north star, the foundation upon which you make decisions, and it helps you not get distracted by noise. As much as you must have a clear goal, whether you are out to save up wealth to see you through retirement, to finance further education of a child, or even expand your savings, a clear picture of what you are out to achieve will still hold you down.

After determining your goals, it is necessary to form a diversified portfolio that matches your risk tolerance. Diversification will protect you against market turbulence by allocating your money to different classes of assets to ensure that no single company can have a tremendous effect on your portfolio. This is not only a strategy that will facilitate mitigating the risk, but also facilitate long-term steady growth. It is important to know the ratio between risk and reward and align your portfolio to that relationship.

Changes in markets are unavoidable, and it is in such moments that one is most tempted to move out of the plans. Due to emotional reaction towards the immediacy of change in the market system, one can tend to make hasty choices, the use of panic sales in the downswing process, or market speculation when the stock market goes up, being examples. To offset this, you must have a rulebook or protocol on how you approach your investment. Such regulations must be founded on the preset strategy and contain some criteria to purchase, hold, and sell investments.

Automating your investments would be one of the good methods of compliance with your plan. Automated contributions to your investment accounts bring emotion out of the choices you make and help make your investments stable and aligned with your vision for the long term. The automation process is useful in disciplining oneself, in an otherwise volatile scenario in the market when one is prone to swaying with feelings and emotions.

Rebalancing your portfolio and vetting it on a regular basis is also a very important part of remaining on the plan. This can be done by reviewing your asset allocation every once in a while to make sure that it matches your investment goals. When assets whose performance has been good are sold and those that have not performed are bought, rebalancing may go on to ensure that you continue at your preferred level of risk and returns. It is a systematic process to make sure that your portfolio aligns with your original strategy.

Lastly, it is crucial to develop patience and a long-term orientation mindset. Investing is not a short-term venture but a long-term process to create wealth. Investors also need to stick to their plans even in the face of short-term results by concentrating on the task at hand instead. Such a change of mindset involves avoiding the temptation to make responses to the day-to-day movements in the market and rather believing in your established strategy.

Finally, discipline, patience, and a clear vision of what you want to do with your money are important in order to invest the way you expect. The solution to dealing with market volatility, through automation of investments, reviewing a portfolio on a regular basis, and having a long-term outlook, will allow anyone to cope with market instabilities and progress towards becoming financially independent.

CHAPTER 13: MONITORING AND REVIEWING YOUR PORTFOLIO

Regular Portfolio Reviews

This is the case because, in the world of investing in the stock market, the landscape is fluid. Economic indicators, company performances, and market conditions keep changing. It is against this backdrop that routine portfolio reviews can be considered essential to an investor, especially to those who are at a very early stage in an investment in the stock market. It is impossible to overestimate the role of such reviews because they are a definite benchmark for maintaining and improving the investment portfolio.

The major key to frequent portfolio reviewing is the notion of alignment. Investors usually come into the market with definite financial objectives, tolerance to risks, and investment plans. However, these factors can change over time as individual circumstances change or on a macroeconomic level. Reviews carried out routinely provide a chance to examine how the existing portfolio fits with such shifting goals. Viewing asset allocations and comparing them with the initial target, an investor will be able to make a proper decision whether to keep the same direction or make certain adjustments.

In addition, periodic review of the portfolio helps in putting up a structure with the help of which the performance of individual investments is analyzed. Markets are not always predictable, and every investment does not works as planned. Systematic reviews provide investors with an opportunity to understand which assets may be performing poorly and whether they ought to continue being included in the strategy. This will mean an examination of several key performance indicators, including return on investment, volatility, and dividend yield. Such evaluations assist in developing tactical decisions of retaining, selling, or even expanding securities within various positions.

Risk management is another important issue of periodic portfolio reviews. The stock market is a risky business to begin with, and it can be affected in a number of ways, resulting in profits or losses. Checking up on the portfolio at regular intervals allows investors to gauge the extent of risk they have been exposed to and what they can do to reduce it. This may mean investing in several asset categories, sectors, or even geographical locations. Risk diversification is a famous way of allocating the risk across all areas and making regular checks on the portfolio to ensure it has not become excessively concentrated in one region.

Tax issues also come into play when reviewing the portfolio. Investments increase and change, so do the tax implications attach to them. Ongoing reviews enable the investor to plan strategically in terms of taxes, where they can use line items such as tax-loss harvesting to increase taxes by comparing gains to losses so as to minimize the overall taxation performance of the portfolio. Knowledge of the tax impacts of the investment decision makes sure that the investor can maximize his or her after-tax returns.

Moreover, periodic portfolio analysis provides an opportunity to keep track of the changes in the market and available opportunities. The market of investing is dynamic, and it keeps evolving continually, and new industries and technologies offer promising opportunities. Monitoring these changes with the help of high-quality reviews will enable the investors to use new opportunities and restructure their portfolios.

Finally, periodic portfolio review is not a mechanical procedure alone, but rather a proactive formula towards improving the results of the investment. They ask the investors to be hungry, knowledgeable, and flexible, components that are very essential in stock market survival over a long period. By engaging in frequent reviews, an investor will have a better chance to deal with the intricacies of the market with certainty and conviction, which means that his or her portfolio will be strong and reflective of his or her financial goals.

Adjusting Your Strategy

When you get further into the realm of investing, it is essential to keep in mind that the strategies that served you best at the starting point of your investing may require certain changes, even with the accumulation of your experience and a shift in financial situation. The central role of this flexibility is to succeed in the stock market in the long term.

When starting, most new investors opt to go the easy, lazy route, usually either investing in index funds or ETFs of a wide market. It is a great option for individuals who are new to the business and may lack time or experience in active trading. Nevertheless, once you gain more knowledge about the market and you are more certain about yourself, you might want to commit to more active strategies. Such a transition may mean buying small portions of stocks, discovering new areas you are enthusiastic about, or even considering entering the world of dividend-oriented investments.

Revisiting your financial goal is one of the initial actions that you can take to reevaluate your strategy. You need to know well what you desire your investments to accomplish. Do you want to create a nest egg that you use to retire, get passive income, or maybe save money to buy a house? Depending on your aims, you will make changes in your investment strategy. As an example, if you are aiming to earn an income, you may need to consider allocating part of your portfolio to dividend-paying securities or funds.

Your risk tolerance is also critical to consider. The more you learn about the market. The more you might change your comfort level in terms of risk. The more people gain, the more risk-averse some of the investors may be, and others may be willing to take more risk to get more returns. Re-evaluating your risk tolerance regularly will help you make sure that your investment plan meets your present financial status and the level of psychological comfort you feel at the moment.

Diversification is another important feature of strategy change. This is particularly true as you have an expanding portfolio; it is important not to be over-weighted in any one category (sector or asset type). Diversifying will reduce risk and flatten returns over time. This could be investing in foreign markets, obtaining bonds, or even getting into other investments such as properties or commodities.

Additionally, being aware and educated of the market trends and other economic indicators may also be helpful in providing hints as to how and when to change your approach. To improve your awareness of the market trends and learn how to make informed decisions, you may read the financial news, watch webinars, or join investment communities.

Lastly, it is crucial to keep in mind that strategy change is not a characteristic of a single occasion, but rather an ongoing activity. It is worthwhile to set a review schedule of your portfolio and strategy, maybe quarterly or annually. Through such a regular check-up, you will also be able to assess how well you have achieved what you wanted and thus make adjustments. It is also a chance to re-allocate your portfolio so as to make sure that it fits your risk tolerance and goals in terms of finance.

To conclude, rebalancing your portfolio is also an essential aspect of efficient investing. It involves thinking about your aims, risk acceptance, and market situation, and being willing to learn and adjust to these. Aiming to meet your financial goals, you can overcome the difficulties of the stock market by operating flexibly and actively.

Performance Metrics to Track

The performance metrics are very important to every investor who intends to enter the stock market. These are the metrics, and they are the guiding torch that helps investors gauge potential and the well-being of investments. With the concentration on particular numbers, newbies will be able to make their choices without the $%6xf where to start syndrome that can happen due to the ocean of statistical information.

Revenue is possibly one of the most basic metrics to understand. Revenue is the overall amount of income that a business generates. It is a direct measure of how well a company is capable of making sales, and in most cases, it becomes the point of reference when analyzing the financial well-being of a company. The presence of revenue growth over the period may demonstrate the expansion of the company as well as the demand for its services or goods in the market.

The other key measurement is profit, also known as the net income. This amount is that which is left behind after subtracting all expenditures from the revenue. Profitability will determine how a company is performing in terms of controlling its costs as well as its capacity to convert sales to real profit. An investor ought to find a company that has a stable or increasing profit margin since it indicates good management and efficiency in operations.

Another big indicator is debt, especially the debt-to-equity ratio. This ratio is the ratio of the total debt available to the company against the shareholders' equity of the company, and it gives a better picture of how the company is funding its operations, by using debt or self-owned funds. The higher debt-to-equity ratio indicates that the company substantially depends on borrowing, which may be dangerous unless it is properly managed, especially during the volatile market conditions.

Another measure of performance to consider is cash flow. It is a gauge of the inflows and outflows of cash in a business; in other words, it is an indication of how successful a business is at settling its short-term debts. A positive cash flow shows that the business has enough finances to sustain its expenditures and to reinvest in its expansion, and a negative cash flow may be a warning signal of a prospective liquidity problem.

One of the most well-liked measures of value is the price-to-earnings (P/E) ratio. It is a measurement of the current price of a company against the company's earnings per share (EPS). A low P/E may imply that a stock is underpriced, and a high P/E indicates that the investors are anticipating more growth in the future. Context is important, however, since when P/E ratios are compared, they must be in the same industry, to be of any real value.

Meanwhile, another useful indicator for those with an interest in income investments is the dividend yield. It can be determined by dividing the annual value of the dividend per share by the price per share. Having a high dividend yield may be appealing as it pumps in a constant income, but one should make sure that the dividend is not a regular occurrence. High yields may indicate the risk or a sign of company distress.

Finally, the return on equity (ROE) is an indicator of the effectiveness with which shareholders' equity is utilized by the management in order to make profits. An increase in ROE shows that the company is efficiently using equity capital, and this is a good sign to investors.

These are some of the major performance measures that a novice can apply to overcome the noise and make decisions. These measurements are able to give an overview of the financial well-being and growth rate of a company, which helps investors to gain an assessment and understand how to look out for investment offers that are likely to appear.

Keeping Up with Market Changes

The stock market world is a dynamic world in which every investor must be sensitive to change. Markets are affected by a great number of factors, including economic indicators and geopolitical events, and all these factors may change rather quickly. The way to cope with changes is by being well aware of the pulse of the market and acting swiftly with the right decisions.

Being able to find time to observe the market on a regular basis is one of the initial steps towards adapting to the market changes. It does not only mean monitoring stock prices but also having a good grip on the wider economic conditions that are behind the changes. Economic reports, including the statistics of employment and inflation, and the growth of GDP, can easily be used to work out trends in the market. Also, such aspects as the policy of the central bank and fluctuations of interest rates may change sentiments on the market significantly.

The investors should also monitor geopolitical issues because such issues may cause volatility in the market. The global markets, in most cases, are affected by the ripple effect of trade negotiations, political elections, and international conflicts. Monitoring news and the opinions of specialists can also assist investors in predicting changes that might occur in the market and transforming their strategies accordingly.

Innovations and technological improvements are of great significance in the dynamics of the market as well. The emergence of online currencies, for example, has created new parameters in the financial world. Learning more about the existing promising technologies and how they might affect various industries can give an investor a competitive advantage. Following the trends in the technology sector can enable the investor to identify new investment opportunities and avoid the risks caused by disruptive innovations.

Additionally, the actions of the market players can affect market movements in a twofold manner. Market changes cannot be avoided without understanding the psychology of an investor, his/her typical biases, and emotional responses. By way of example, fear and panic feelings during a market decline may cause a massive sell-off of stocks, and optimism during bull markets may cause stocks to be overvalued. Being aware of those patterns, it is possible to keep a level-headed attitude and prevent knee-jerking.

Diversification is one of the strategies to manage change in the market well. Investors are able to diversify their investments in terms of types of assets and sectors, and through this, they are able to cushion the effects of negative market trends. Diversification plays a role in reducing the risk of having a single form of investment and also permits steady returns in the long run.

Also, it is vital to keep abreast by means of constant learning. Even reading financial articles, joining a webinar, and attending investment seminars can add to the knowledge of an investor about how the market works. Other investors and investment communities can also be a source of good ideas and encouragement, but networking with other investors is key.

Finally, investors should ensure that they occasionally check and change their portfolios. Periodic reviews of the portfolio are useful in revising investments and tailoring them to a fluctuating market and financial objectives. Rebalancing of these portfolios prevents the effects of market volatility so that the desired asset allocations are maintained and an investor can be financially healthy.

As can be summed up, it is not a matter of keeping up with the evolutions going on in the market, but it is also about responding to the changes with one's head and a big picture mind. Is it possible that by establishing a deep insight into the economy and economic indicators, geopolitical events, technological trends, and investor dynamics, investors are able to tread the treacherous waters of the stock market with assurance and a strength of their own?

CHAPTER 14: CONTINUOUS LEARNING AND GROWTH

Resources for Ongoing Education

Further learning in stock market investment is priceless, providing new and experienced investors a way into the path that will allow them to widen their knowledge and perfect their combination. There are plentiful sources to facilitate this continuing process of learning, and each is addressed to fulfill various dimensions of the investment in knowledge and skills development.

Online media is one of the sources of consistent learning. To be in line with the current trends and market developments, information is imported through websites such as Yahoo Finance and Morningstar, which offer free information and news. Morningstar can be the ideal source of fundamental information on fund analysis that a prospective investor may want to gain insight into the in-depth information on fund analysis. In the meantime, Investopedia is one of the resources that makes it easy to find definitions and tutorials, and complicated financial terms are simplified into easy-to-understand concepts.

Books are a resource of all times that can be used as a source of advanced learning. The book is an excellent recommendation and has mostly to do with index investing, which gives a simple form that matches the idea of simplicity in investing. Another great book is called Broke Millennial Takes on Investing by Erin Lowry, and it is definitely worth reading, especially if you are a young professional who wants to get advice regarding the investment world that is close to you.

Podcasts and YouTube channels provide active and entertaining information in the sphere of audio and visual learning. Bigger Pockets Money Podcast offers information and inspiring personal finance and investing stories. In contrast, Animal Spirits offers a laid-back market commentary, which is informative and entertaining at the same time. Listeners get to be educated by these platforms and be more critical of how they want to make investments.

The development of a custom-made 30-day challenge is outright life-changing to one who is particular as far as learning is concerned. This difficulty can be addressed by the creation of weekly objectives like analyzing investment plans, making paper trades, and recording performance in a journal. This type of systematic pattern is going to promote the formation of regular patterns of investing and provide a possibility to transfer the theoretical knowledge into practice.

As far as continuous learning is concerned, there is also the role of communities and forums. Participation in peer-supported communities, such as r/personal finance or the Bogle heads forum, gives an opportunity to spend time on Q&A, to share experiences, and learn about other people's experiences. Through these platforms, investors can find support and common ground as the platforms provide the feeling of a community where an investor can discuss his or her approach and do better calculations.

Besides, it is important to devote some time to education. Spending only 30 minutes a week on listening to a new podcast or any article can drastically increase the level of knowledge in the long term. Study can also be enhanced through monthly updates or questions in one of the selected forums, in which one can have the opportunity for reflection and development.

Therefore, as a conclusion, successful investing is the key to never ceasing to learn and adapt. The availability of many resources, including online tools and books, podcasts, and community forums, can help investors always be informed, polish their plan, and eventually realize their financial desires. Such a determined investment in continuous learning not only increases investment savvy but also instills confidence and strength in maneuvering in the financial market, which is rapidly changing.

Joining Investment Communities

The importance of community cannot be underestimated in the context of stock market investing. To new investors, participation in investment communities can be an important step on the way to becoming confident and informed. Such (online or offline) communities provide a platform where the community members can share their experiences, discuss the strategy, and learn from the successes and failures of each other.

The sense of accountability and support network is important. It could be essential when it comes to a sense of focus and motivation, which is gained through engaging in investment communities. The amount of information that a learner can come across can be so much to disturb many beginners, and a community can assist many to find their way and feel less alone. A good place to start would be an online subreddit like r/personal finance or the Bogle heads subreddit, where one can get help with anything related to personal finance, as well as strategies to use index funds. Such platforms are full of threads and even Q&A sessions in which the topic is specifically on learning, and people can pose questions without the fear of anybody judging them.

It is also easy to join these groups. First, start by ascertaining similar communities with your investment objectives and philosophy. Seek the ones that focus on education, disclosure, and care. As soon as you identify a community worth your time, the first step is registration. First, you may prefer to lurk-watch what people act and talk about, get a feel of how the community works, and what kind of things get discussed frequently. This is the time of observation, which enables you to absorb any information and determine the setting and standard of advice that is offered.

When you are comfortable, begin by actively participating through discussions. Write comments about your experiences, ask questions, and consult on certain areas that are topics of concern to you. The aim is to learn and develop, and thus, be open-minded when interacting with people. Appropriate standards of communicating with such communities are to be respectful, focused, and, where necessary, value-adding. It is easy to be carried away by the ideas of your colleagues, but rather, you should use the facts discovered and base your research and decisions on them.

Furthermore, the investment communities provide the possibility of creating smaller and more specific groups, called the mastermind groups or the accountability buddies. Such smaller groups will be beneficial in terms of a more personal approach and support. The habit of meeting with these groups regularly can keep you accountable in terms of your goals and provide a place to report the progress and failures. It can be helpful to place a meeting schedule on it weekly, bi-weekly, or monthly, which may provide consistency and attention.

Filtering out the noise is one of the problems of being a part of an investment community. Different voices express numerous opinions, and it is easy to feel lost due to the tremendous number of voices that help to make sure that popular opinion is popular. To overcome this, set up a system to separate good ideas from good information and solid ideas from mere speculation or hyped claims. Managing peer advice and research with thoughts and independent research is important. Use the strategy of taking notes, but do not plan it out yourself, so that you stay in control of the process of the investment.

After all, being a part of an investment society is basically about learning and evolving with others. It is a matter of capitalizing on the combined wisdom and experience of the community to boost your knowledge and expertise. No need to look far to get an answer regarding the fundamentals of stock market investing or a tip-off on how you can improve your strategy, these communities of like-minded individuals can offer you constant assistance and advice in a surrounding that is growing steadily more complex.

Learning from Experienced Investors

The same can be said about the world of stock market investing, where the words of wisdom will likely be the words of those who have already walked the road, we tread. Beginners can greatly benefit by watching and learning the strategy and lessons applied by successful investors. These experienced people have seen both the downs and the ups of the market and have passed the stage of trial and error, and their experiences are worth a treasure chest of lessons.

Patience is one of the biggest things that veteran investors can teach you. When you enter the stock market, you are not in a get-rich-quick situation; rather, you are in it as a long-term business, and it will pay off with patience. Successful investors realize that the volatility in any market is normal when investing. They have witnessed the market climb up and crash down and have learnt not to be in a panic mode during its downturn. Instead, they take such times as a chance to purchase high-quality stocks at low prices. This is due to the fact that this patience is accompanied by a clear insight about what the market is like; in that, it is the consistent, steadfast person whose investment approach would always be rewarded over time.

The importance of diversification is also another piece of knowledge that experienced investors can provide. They diversify their investments by holding a mix of assets; they invest in multiple classes and sectors, and thus they reduce their risk exposure and stabilize returns. Diversification brings about the fact that a bad result in one aspect is offset by a good result in the other. This is another key characteristic of sound investment, and it is frequently stressed by people who have lots of experience in the market. As they are aware, when you put all the eggs in one basket, you end up losing a lot of them and becoming stressed.

In addition, skilled investors emphasize that it is always necessary to learn and evolve. The stock market is dynamic, and it is affected by economic changes, advancements in technology, and geopolitical factors. Experienced investors are well aware of such changes and adjust their strategies accordingly. They read a lot, monitor market tendencies, and are continually searching for new opportunities. This is the eminent desire to learn that keeps them on their toes and enables them to make informed decisions.

The second area that experienced investors have mastered is that of risk management. They are perfect in risk evaluation, and they plan to reduce losses caused by such risks. They take what they know, and they are willing to take the risk they can take and continue investing, and usually use stop-loss orders as a safeguard for their investments. This reduction of risk by the discipline ensures that they do not discount on emotions or current market changes.

Senior investors are also people who are devoted to networking and community participation. They tend to join investment groups or use such forums on the Internet, where idea exchange and learning with each other are possible. This type of teamwork does not just expand their knowledge, but also helps them to gain substance and receive encouragement.

Finally, some of the seasoned investor's stress that it is useful to create definite, attainable goals. They actually see the clear picture of what they want to become and come up with an idea on how to attain those objectives. It can be saving towards retirement, creating a college fund, or becoming financially independent, but having a definite goal to pursue makes them focused and motivated.

In summary, experience is an excellent source of knowledge and insights on how to succeed in investing, which can be applied by an inexperienced investor. New investors can make it an excellent foundation for their investment experience by endeavoring to embrace the values of good and diligent practice (like patience, diversification, continuous learning, risk management, networking, and goal setting) that the older investors have used.

Staying Motivated and Persistent

When it comes to investing in the stock market, motivation and persistence are important elements in the process of long-term success. Life can be full of twists and turns, and how one manages to remain firm in the Friday moments is what other people can learn. The attitude that one should adopt, especially when learning a new subject, is being able to learn through mistakes and looking at disappointments as a space to learn. Such a method not only makes the business resilient but also helps to understand the market better.

Another good tip in managing motivation is to set realistic goals. This is done through the setting of certain milestones through which investors can monitor their progress and be allowed to feel small wins as they go along. The practice is not only accomplishing but can also strengthen the behaviors that result in success. One should keep in mind that investing is a marathon, and patience is crucial. Since it takes into account the big picture together with long-term goals, investors do not have to give in to temptations to make a rushed decision on the current fluctuations of the market.

The second element of remaining motivated is never-ending education. The stock market changes constantly, and the knowledge of new trends, technologies, and methods can make an investor active and interested in the process of investing. It is possible to subscribe to trustworthy sources of financial news, attend webinars, and even invest in investment forums, which will help gather valuable insights and make as person feel part of the community. It can also be encouraging to interact with other investors, and this can help, especially when one is going through tough times.

Moreover, to stay more motivated and persistent, it may be a great idea to have a routine, as well as to receive an education. Setting up an effective routine of checking portfolios, searching for new potentials, and reviewing the decisions made on investments may make a person feel disciplined and control-oriented. Such a habit enables investors to keep themselves concentrated on their objectives, and they are less likely to make hasty decisions when the markets are subject to fluctuations. When you work on a project, it is also a good way to have a regular break and a period of reflection, to rejuvenate oneself and have a positive outlook.

Besides, it is important to avoid and control emotions. The stock market is volatile and can be rash at times, which can lead to bad decisions. By establishing ways to deal with the stress, investors can calm down and focus by meditating or writing in a journal, etc. It is often advisable to identify emotional buttons and always have a channel of response in case one feels they are emotionally unsettled, because emotions are often the root of impulsive decisions that would rarely serve in the long term.

Lastly, you need to put everything into perspective and hold in mind the reasoning that has led you to invest in the first place. It can be getting free of money, saving to see out old age, or developing a legacy, but having that end-goal in your sights can help get you through rough patches. This may be done by going back over your original goals and looking at what you have accomplished so that hope and dedication can be rekindled.

To summarize, nearly all of the above can be applied to maintain motivation and perseverance in investing in the stock market; it is primarily composed of goal setting, ongoing learning, routine maintenance, emotional control, and point of view. These strategies will help the investors to swim through the intricacy of the market with confidence and strength, to reach their goals of financial gain.

www.ingramcontent.com/pod-product-compliance
Lightning Source LLC
Chambersburg PA
CBHW070929210326
41520CB00021B/6863